BAPTIZE BY BLAZING HOLY FIRE

-The Secret Room-

BAPTIZE BY BLAZING FIRE BOOK 3

YONG-DOO KIM

Baptize by Blazing Fire by Yong-Doo Kim
Published by Fire of God Ministries
42776 Albrae St. Fremont, CA 94538
www.fireofgod.church

Copyright@2017 by Yong-Doo Kim
All rights reserved

Global Headquarters - Lord's Church South Korea
Pastor Yong-Doo Kim, Email: y6475@hanmail.net

An International Holy Fire Ministry
Branch Churches in United States of America

Fire of God Ministries - Lord's Church San Francisco/Fremont, CA
Pastor Steve & Yoojin Kim
42776 Albrae St, Fremont, CA 94538
Tel) 209-747-5868
www.fireofGod.Church
Fire of God Ministries translated all six books of Pastor Kim, Yong Doo, "Baptize By Blazing Fire". Fire of God is responsible for all salient translations of Pastor Kim, Yong Doo's sermons/messages.

The Lord's Church of Minnesota
Pastor Thao & Bao Xiong
Tel) 651-600-4076

The Lord's Church of Los Angeles
Pastor Sungjee & Seounghee Cho
8611 Roland St. Suite F, Buena Park, Ca 90621
Tel) 714-388-7736
Pastor Sungjee Cho is travel and media administrator to Pastor Kim, Yong Doo. Pastor Cho arranges and assists in scheduling revival meetings, airfares, hotels, car rental, and also is in charge of media production. He is the photographer and video personal during the revival meetings.

The Lord's Church of Georgia
Pastor Elijah & Youngsook Park
3751 Venture Dr. #260B, Duluth, Ga 30096
Tel) 678-862-9329

Book cover image by Wonju Hulse www.wonju-hulse.fineartamerica.com

This book records the true spiritual experiences of
the members of The Lord's Church in
So Incheon, South Korea 2005.

During 30 days of continual midnight prayer at a small Korean Church, the congregation experienced an unbelievable revival. With their hands raised up, and praying all night long, the congregation had their spiritual eyes opened as they experienced visions, healing, intense spiritual warfare, and transforming encounters with Jesus.

There are 6 books in the series, this is book 3.

CONTENTS

Chapter 1: Walking through the twelve pearly doors
February 9th, 2005 (Wednesday)
February 10th, 2005 (Thursday)
February 11th, 2005 (Friday)
February 14th, 2005 (Monday)
February 15th, 2005 (Tuesday)

Chapter 2: Holy Spirit's Poisonous Thorn
February 17th, 2005 (Thursday)
February 18th, 2005 (Friday)
February 19th, 2005 (Saturday)
February 21st, 2005 (Monday)
February 25th, 2005 (Friday)

Chapter 3: Holy Electricity
February 28th, 2005 (Monday)
March 4th, 2005 (Friday)
March 6th, 2005 (Sunday)
March 9th, 2005 (Wednesday)
March 10th, 2005 (Thursday)

Chapter 4: The Secret Room
March 12th, 2005 (Saturday)
March 13th, 2005 (Sunday)
March 15th, 2005 (Tuesday)
March 25th, 2005 (Friday)
April 10th, 2005 (Sunday Evening)

Chapter 5: Visiting Heaven In A Group With The Lord
April 15th, 2005 (Friday)
April 16th, 2005 (Saturday Night)
April 17th, 2005 (Sunday Evening)
April 20th, 2005 (Wednesday)

Chapter 1
Walking Through The Twelve Pearly Doors

February 9th, 2005 (Wednesday): "Accomplishing blessings in the New Year"

Sermon scriptures: "Thus saith the LORD the maker thereof, the LORD that formed it, to establish it; the LORD is his name; call unto me, and I will answer thee, and show thee great and mighty things, which thou knowest not." (Jeremiah 33:2-3) KJV.

1. God And Our Relationship

When God speaks His word has a front and a back. Just as there is the palm and the back of the hand as well as a head and a tail on a coin, there are double meanings to His word.

Those who receive the Lord's word with faith will receive the promise of salvation and be blessed with the eternal life. But, if you are filled with unbelief and disobey Him you will face many trials and tribulations. Just as the Israelites often forgot about God, and when they rejected His invitation to be the chosen nation, they suffered through many wars and were taken as the enemy's prisoners. Their lives were filled with misery and they experienced many devastating sufferings.

Therefore, the believers must be certain that their relationship is thoroughly joined with God specifically during the times of distress and adversity. Also, in our walk with Christ we must be devoted with all our hearts, with certainty and with a positive attitude to bring joy to our Lord. Our God the Father never overlooks rebuking His children's shortcomings. As if playing with a spinning top, the more one fearfully whips the top, it spins correctly and balances. As such, it is imperative for us to know if our relationship with God is that of salvation and eternal life or curse and judgment.

2. God Fulfills And Completes His Work

God is a planner and designer of a divine plan. He is concerned about us humans, and is constantly thinking and working for our well being. Therefore, the Bible describes our God as a potter who makes various potteries out of clay (Isaiah 45:9).

Before creating a clay bowl, a potter plans ahead and molds the clay with his bare hands and a potter never makes anything unprepared. A potter is deeply devoted and concentrates on the project until it"s perfectly completed. Then when the project turns out to be a masterpiece, all are filled with admiration and delight.

"I form the light, and create darkness: I make peace, and create evil: I the LORD do all these things" (Isaiah 45:7) KJV. You and I are the precious masterpiece that God has personally created.

The various appearances of our faces and personalities are all different and we are sent into this world with our uniqueness. No one can dare to imitate such creation and we are the most precious souls in this world. Consequently, it is wrong to put ourselves down, but it is also wrong to lift ourselves up above our creator, and become arrogant. We must always give thanksgiving and glory to the Lord.

3. Cry Out To God And Pray

We can say that one of the most important aspects of human life is the exchange of words between people. Communication is an important step in understanding the inner thoughts of others. God said if we want to know His thoughts, He urges us to open our mouths, cry out and pray. Then He promises to share the secret no one else knows.

The new and the old testaments are filled with people's cries and prayers and God"s answers to those earnest prayers. Whether as a group, a family, or individually, when we pray out loud and cry out to God we will always receive the proper answers to the matter at hand. God takes the opportunity to personally intervene when we are fervently crying out to him. The Bible states that when we cry out to God he will say, "Here I am" (Isaiah 58:9) KJV and the Lord is never far away, but is always near.

Jeremiah, as a prophet, spent his lifetime crying out for his nation and people. But, if it was not Jeremiah who prayed to God, God would have chosen someone else to take Jeremiah's place. When we study the prophets and their work in the Bible, we see their lives were lived exclusively as servants of God.

God is always looking for people who fit appropriately for the particular time frame we live in. When He finds the right servant, He will give the power, and the Holy Spirit will pour down the anointing oil utilizing the individual mightily. How each is used depends on the size of their spiritual bowl, but we must be thankful that we are called by God to be used; therefore, we must faithfully devote ourselves to that call.

In this life we can be used by God for a short moment or our lives can be used entirely until death. On that account, if we want to be used for a long time we must live according to His plan without changing. "But in a great house there are not only vessels of gold and of silver, but also of wood and of earth; and some to honor, and some to dishonour. If a man therefore purge himself from these, he shall be a vessel unto honour, sanctified, and meet for the master's use, and prepared unto every good work" (2 Timothy 2:20-21) KJV.

4. I Will Reveal My Secrets

"Surely the Lord GOD will do nothing, but he revealeth his secret unto his servants the prophets. The lion hath roared, who will not fear? The Lord GOD hath spoken, who can but prophesy?" (Amos

3:7-8) KJV.

Our God the Father reveals His secrets to those who diligently seek and knock. God's secret can be taken away by those who are faithfully and passionately seeking, which stirs our curiosity and at the same time motivates us. Faith, along with the word, prayer, and diligently desiring to be in the presence of the Lord is when the secret will be revealed to you.

This truth certainly shows an enormous grace of our Lord. There can be many interpretations of what it means to reveal the secrets, but deviating from the original meaning, there is also "passing the test through a deep, grieving prayer," interpreting the mystery, that is

"It will be revealed with much information," and this is what it means. Actually, the Lord showed me many events that are still yet to occur. "And he said, I will make all my goodness pass before thee, and I will proclaim the name of the LORD before thee; and will be gracious to whom I will be gracious, and will shew mercy on whom I will shew mercy" (Exodus 33:19) KJV.

God the Father does not simply give to us the enormous volume of spiritual secrets, but through various large and small trials and tests they are revealed. The Lord's inspection of our readiness is experienced every day in our spiritual as well as our physical livelihood. However, what's more painful and difficult is the fact that God does not warn us ahead of time and we absolutely have no clue regarding when, where, and with what method the test will progress. This is why we cannot be free from tension and we must always pray without ceasing. "And from the days of John the Baptist until now the kingdom of heaven suffereth violence, and the violent take it by force" (Matthew 11:12) KJV.

God is seeking for souls who will approach the kingdom of heaven, and unlock the spiritual secrets. Then in the end times He will use them as the workers for the harvest to harvest the grains. For this work we must endure until the Lord's approval of our readiness and seek deeper and pray through continual, endless, humble, and powerful faith.

The way God is currently dealing with our church is exceptionally uncommon compared to other churches. The reason is because it has to do with what will take place in the end times; there will be views strongly affirming and those who are uncertain. When we look back at our nation's shocking experience in the past, it is most likely the majority of opinions will be negative. This is why the subject is dealt with cautiously and seriously.

Today, we are spiritually blinded and the more we proceed forward, the more uncertain the world becomes. This is why the Lord baptized us with the Holy Spirit and fire — revealing the power of the Lord to save the lost souls. "I indeed baptize you with water unto repentance. But he that cometh after me is mightier than I, whose shoes I am not worthy to bear: he shall baptize you with the Holy Ghost, and with fire" (Matthew 3:11) KJV.

We are experiencing the blazing baptism of the Holy Spirit on a daily basis. No matter where the location we are at, the Lord's power is upon us when two or more of us are gathered together. "And this is the confidence that we have in him, that, if we ask any thing according to his will, he heareth us" (1 John 5:14) KJV, and this is His promise. We are certain that we can be renewed daily through prayer. Hallelujah!

* Regarding The Guardian Angels

In the Bible there is no mention of the "guardian" angels. Instead, Apostle Peter mentions briefly in Acts 12:15 of such an angel. The concepts of the guardian angels often arouse our curiosity of the Bible. "Which things also we speak, not in the words which man's wisdom teacheth, but which the Holy Ghost teacheth; comparing spiritual things with spiritual" (1 Corinthians 2:13) KJV.

Those of us who are Christians would like to know if the guardian angels truly exist. Generally, those with the spiritual gift of distinction who have stepped into the spiritual realm know the truth, and we're sharing the real experience with the world. The spiritual events can only be distinguished spiritually, and Jesus commanded that we inform the spiritually unaware Christians with certainty and record precisely what was revealed.

* Kim, Joo-Eun Meets The Guardian Angel

Kim, Joo-Eun: A week after the New Year I went to my maternal grandparents" house. My grandfather and grandmother greeted me joyfully. My pastor and father said, "Joo-Eun, right now your grandpa and grandma will be reciting the sinner's prayer of repentance, so observe carefully with you spiritual eyes," and then he began preparing for prayer. My father asked my grandparents to kneel down and repeat the prayer after him.

They both repeated, "Our heavenly Father, I am a sinner. I did not know you and lived until now worshipping an idol. Please forgive me of my sins! From now on I will accept and worship your son Jesus Christ as my savior." And when they prayed, God sent two angels to descend from heaven who took their places besides my grandparents. The two angels were my grandparents" guardian angels who will protect them until the end.

As soon as the angels descended from heaven, they respectfully bowed their heads before Jesus, and by raising one hand they displayed what looked like a gesture of taking a pledge. This scene looked heroic yet humbling. Jesus spoke to them with His glorious and majestic voice. "You have been entrusted with the duty of protecting brother Kang, Soo-Yong, and sister, Haam, Oak-Boon until they depart from this earth. Do you understand?" As soon as the command was given, the angels bowed their heads and bent their knees slightly and respectfully answered, "Yes, my holy Lord! We will do as you said."

But what was peculiar was as soon as they answered, the angels wings disappeared, so I could not help but ask Jesus a question regarding this. "Jesus! When the angels first came down from heaven they had wings, but why did their wings suddenly disappear?" Jesus explained, "My dear Sesame, don't you have such a curious mind? The angel's wings did not disappear."

* The Angel's Wings And Feathers

"The guardian angels's wings and their feathers have a close connection to the believer's faith. When the believers live devoted and faithfully to me, the angels's wings will begin to grow, and later it will become a large wing. Also, the feathers on the wings will grow beautifully." "Oh I see, Lord! Thank you for explaining it to me." When I showed my gratitude toward Jesus, He smiled and was very pleased.

Jesus told me that in heaven my mother's paternal and maternal grandmothers are with us today celebrating my maternal grandparents accepting salvation, and the Lord promised to bring them my mother's grandmothers to the Lord's Church service.

When I relayed this information to the pastor he excitedly said, "Joo-Eun! That is a sensitive issue so we have to be cautious talking about it. It can bring about enormous adverse criticisms from many churches around our nation." As soon as the pastor finished his thoughts, Jesus, who was standing beside me said, "Is there anything that I can't do? Pastor Kim do not worry yourself sick! I have invited many souls from heaven to join the service at the Lord's Church, and it is because your service is focused on me and spiritually alive. In the near future I plan to take many of my well known servants from the Bible to personally witness the sermon at the Lord's Church, and those congregational members with the gift of spiritual sight will clearly see and have conversations with them."

Filled with overwhelming excitement I gazed at Jesus, shouting, "Wow! Jesus! Does that mean our forefathers of faith, Abraham, Moses and Elijah will be attending our church service?" Jesus replied, "Yes, yes. Of course, yes! Right now they are all looking forward to visiting the Lord's Church."

As soon as I got home I shared this with my brother, Joseph, and he immediately responded, "Wow! Then I will like to meet and talk to Job's daughters first." When I heard that I was jealous. Jesus once again gave me His word to remind my father to record precisely what transpired today.

* The Process Of Receiving Jesus

"That if thou shalt confess with thy mouth the Lord Jesus, and shalt believe in thine heart that God hath raised him from the dead, thou shalt be saved. For with the heart man believeth unto righteousness; and with the mouth confession is made unto salvation" (Romans 10:9-10) KJV.

Jesus explained, "Sesame! In order for someone to be saved, they must believe and receive me sincerely deep into their hearts, but most importantly it is crucial to have a sincere heart and mind. Many who have received me end up in hell, because during the prayer of confession they simply recited the prayer without sincerity!"

Jesus also said, "Many profess they have accepted and proclaimed me into their hearts, and with their mouths believe that they are saved, since they've believed in me for a long time, but, it is not the length of time that determines your salvation. It is the process of bearing fruits in your character that leads you closer to attaining salvation. Many believe blindly the incorrect teaching that simply reciting with their mouths will guarantee their salvation — and are under an illusion that they will go to heaven. Salvation should be realized through fear and trembling and each individual must grow in sincere faith." Jesus is heartbroken and frustrated that so many souls end up in hell because they believed erroneously.

I asked Jesus, "Jesus! What do I do? Can I receive salvation?" and Jesus, filled with grace, responded, "Yes, of course. Why wouldn't my Sesame receive salvation? But, you also must diligently obey and live faithfully. Do you understand?" I made a promise and said "Yes, Lord! I will live as you said."

"Wherefore, my beloved, as ye have always obeyed, not as in my presence only, but now much more in my absence, work out your own salvation with fear and trembling" (Philippians 2:12). "Receiving the end of your faith, even the salvation of your souls" (1 Peter 1:9) KJV.

* Joseph Finally Encounters The Female Demon

Kim, Joseph: I was concentrating on pleading with the Lord for the spiritual gift of sight and I was on fire praying in tongues when approximately 3 feet away in front of me there was a person wearing a white garment sitting with their back to me. While I was praying I thought 'Who is this person sitting with their back to me?' It didn't look like the person was a male because the straight hair was tied down long, and it was shaking a little bit. I became really curious and my fear began to grow as well.

I was sure it was a demon, but without budging, it sat with its back facing me. My fear grew even bigger. Suddenly, in that moment with a scream, "Ahhhh!" the demon's head turned backward facing me, and I was sure my heart stopped beating. The female demon twisted her head with its mouth wide opened as the blood poured out profusely from the fangs protruding from the top and the bottom of its mouth. The edge of the demon"s eyes bled as it narrowed its eyes and stared down at me, talking. "I will send you to hell!" When I heard this I was terrified and didn't know what to do, so I began to pray to fight back. "Hey, you filthy demon! In the name of Jesus flee from me! Depart from me!"

But, the demon did not easily retreat. Instead, it attacked me with its sharp nails to scratch me. I often memorized Bible verses to always be prepared for the demon's attacks, so I shouted out, "Submit yourselves therefore to God. Resist the devil, and he will flee from you" (James 4:7) KJV. Even with this, the female demon did not flee because she was a very malicious one. I began to recite loudly Matthew 16:17 filled with authority. "And these signs shall follow them that believe; In my name shall they cast out devils; they shall speak with new tongues." At that moment the demon fled from me for the first time.

I continued to pray after this incident when countless female demons continuously approached me once again. Until now, before my gift of spiritual sight, I often cried and worried that I would never receive the gift. When I first heard how quickly sister Baek, Bong-Nyo, Haak-Sung and Joo-Eun had received their gift of spiritual sight and of their spiritual battles with the demons, I never dreamt that I would be experiencing it for myself. As we can see with our eyes and talk, the demons were clear and certainly visible to our eyes. We can perceive them with all our senses. Demons with missing eyes and sometimes only the eye balls rolled toward me, as well as a blue demon with eyes like a cat, and many female demons continued to attack me, but I gouged each of their eyes out and threw them far away from me.

Then suddenly it was quiet and I couldn't see anything, so I continued to pray in tongues. A gigantic wild boar with sharp fangs from both sides charged toward me, honking loudly, "Honk!" As the hot steam from the boar's nose and mouth hit me, the disgusting stench made me nauseous. Without a warning, when I was totally unprepared, the boar tried to head butt me, so Haak-Sung who was praying beside me shouted, "Joseph, watch out – it's dangerous! Take cover and move!" and with that warning, he confronted and stood face to face with the boar. Brother Haa-Sung took the boar by the neck and forced it onto the ground, then the boar screeched "Honk!" and disappeared.

I let out a sigh, "Whew!" to relieve my tension and began to pray in tongues continuously. This time I saw a large boulder; it was pitch dark everywhere. I began to see something that looked like wolves, and one by one they howled, crying out "Aooooo! Aooooo! Aoooo!" There went the goose bumps again. At the same time, without realizing, an anaconda slithered beside me and began coiling and suffocating me — which happened literally in the blink of an eye.

When it became difficult to breathe, in that moment I thought it will be just a matter of time before I will die, so I kicked and struggled, but I had no energy left in me to scream. Nevertheless, I gathered all my strength: "Lord, Lord! Strengthen me! Give me the strength" and immediately I was filled with mighty strength. I grabbed the anaconda with my hands and threw it far away.

Finally, after defeating the attacks from the demons, I felt as if my prayer suddenly gained some wings and flew at an unbelievable speed toward heaven. I felt it so distinctly. The atmosphere surrounding the earth was slightly reddish yellow and it was so beautiful.

* The Wild Boar Demon

Kim, Joo-Eun: The wild boar demon that appeared violently before my brother, Joseph, began charging toward me and it displayed a gray, ashy color. I was so terrified I opened my eyes, and the boar disappeared. I closed my eyes again and continued praying. There in front of me was a deep forest and I was walking in it alone. Then the boar that I saw a few moments ago reappeared suddenly, charging at me full speed, trying to collide into me. I ran frantically away from the wild boar that was chasing me endlessly, when I saw a wide road ahead and ran into the middle of the road, and there I saw Jesus standing there.

I shouted out to Him, "Jesus, Jesus! Please save me. The wild boar is attacking me!" and I ran into the Lord's arms. The Lord comforted me and said, "Dearest Joo-Eun, do not worry." Jesus then grabbed the charging wild boar, plucked out all its fur, beat it down and the boar cried out in pain. Jesus then threw the wild boar far away from me.

* My House In Heaven

I said, "My beloved Jesus! I want to see my house in heaven. I would like to see it. Please let me see it just once!" and I pleaded with the Lord. At that instant, different scenery unfolded before my eyes to an unbelievable sight where enormous light poured out, so I could not keep my eyes open. The large house at a distant was encased in various shades of pink brilliance. I thought to myself 'I like the color pink, too….wow! I don't know who the owner of this house is, but I am so envious, so very envious.' Jesus held my hand and led me closer to the house and said we should find out whose house it was, so I casually followed Him. I was so happy I thought I was going to faint.

That house was none other than my own, and there was a sign on the side reading "Sesame's house" — my nickname. From afar the house looked pink, but when I got a closer look there were actually many different colors mixed in the brilliance. My house in heaven was so magnificent, large and tall, that when I stood at the front door I felt like a speck of dust. The width was significantly wide as well. Jesus already knew that my favorite color was pink and accordingly has prepared my house with pink brilliance. At the entrance of my house stood two tall angels wearing swords, and when they saw me, they respectfully bowed saying, "Welcome, sister Joo-Eun!" I did not enter the house, but enjoyed only the exterior.

There were so many gems and diamonds I've never seen before stuck into the door and the walls, and when the light shined on them I could not think straight. Some areas of the house were shaped like Lego blocks, and the higher the house went up, blossomed out like a morning glory. I don't know why, but maybe because it was my house that all the other houses looked smaller than mine. I thanked Jesus over and over again. "Jesus, my beloved Jesus! Thank you so very much. It is magnificent and beautiful!" Then Jesus replied, "You're welcome, Joo-Eun! Next time I will take you inside your house, so pray diligently." Also, Jesus promised that when I do something with faith, whatever it is, He will build my house bigger and higher.

* A Prayer That Soars High Up To Heaven

Lee, Haak-Sung: While I was praying, Jesus came to me and He passed between all the praying individuals, and smiled, while mumbling under His breath. "I want to especially see whose prayer will soar highest to heaven, so let's see," and as soon as He said this, every single one of us simultaneously began to pray, trying to be filled with blazing fire of the Holy Spirit. I felt like we were firing a pistol of prayer.

Jesus said aloud, "Let's see. That's right, all right! As expected, Pastor Kim is doing very well! Yes, yes, you're doing great. Be louder, more fire, much more earnestly! Oh yes, you're doing great. Awesome… Sister Kang, Hyun-Ja, and is my bride to be also praying out loud? Yes, that's it!" Then Jesus concentrated on hearing Joseph, Joo-Eun, myself, Yoo-Kyung, my mom, and Deaconess Shin. Jesus passed back and forth among us to examine how high our prayer was traveling. I can see visually that our prayer was like a race and how we performed was intensely displayed as bars on a graph.

February 10th, 2005 (Thursday)

Sermon Passage: "For therein is the righteousness of God revealed from faith to faith: as it is written, the just shall live by faith" (Romans 1:17) KJV.

* Joo-Eun Sees The Entrance Of Hell

Kim, Joo-Eun: I was praying out loud when the shining, luminance of Jesus was approaching toward me. Jesus took my hand and said, "My Sesame! You have to come with me, so follow me." I replied, "Yes, Jesus." As soon as I held onto the Lord's hand, I was traveling along a dark and long tunnel, and I perceived immediately I was in hell.

As usual, the road in hell is always dark and gives me the chills. We walked for a while and as we walked, toward the left side of the road I saw a large arrow clearly before me. At first it seemed the arrow was simply pointing at a certain direction, but soon I realized that there was no other way to go beside the direction the arrow was pointing. When we entered deeper, a clean sign reading, "Hell's Entrance" caught my eyes and at that moment my body began to shrink back. T he Lord quickly read my mind and said, "Joo-Eun, do not worry. I will protect you" and He reassured me.

Entering even further into hell, the road was glowing red, and I couldn't stand the blazing heat. It seemed everything was made hot from the tremendous heat. I endured it as long as possible, but I became more scared and terrified, so I cried out, "Jesus, Jesus! It is too hot and I am scared." The Lord comforted me by reminding me not to worry.

Finally, when the door to the hell opened with the fiery heat, the screams of countless people could be heard all at once. Many small roads stretched out, divided and connected with many other roads, and on both sides of the road were bottomless cliffs. The small and large flames of fire were alive and were climbing up the sides of the cliff. On the left there were many gigantic frying pans with handles on both sides. I've seen many people being cooked alive in the frying pans before, but there is a tremendous size difference with the ones I was seeing. The pan was ten times larger than my elementary athletic field.

The pan was filled with naked bodies and there was so much smoke. The demons began to pour an oil-like substance on the bodies which began to scream and run frantically trying to avoid the grease. Below their feet the pan became red hot from the fire, and from above the demons beat them and poured boiling oil all over them. The people looked like they were clothed in rags, but it was their flesh peeling off in tatters as they gnashed their teeth.

Also, on the other side there was a mountain of a wall and each of the walls were covered with countless holes. These holes were connected as far down to the bottom of the hell, and inside the dark holes were sounds of people screaming continuously. The stench was horrible so I said, "Jesus! I felt sick to my stomach and it's unbearable," so the Lord replied, "Of course, Joo-Eun! I will make sure you can't smell anything." He then touched my nose, allowing me to only see and feel things around me.

Beside the frying pan, I could see the many different demons surrounding it. There were demons resembling an old woman, short haired, white haired skulls, various species of snakes, and demons with animal heads, those with bat's wings that were flying around, as well as countless other demons. Every single one of these demons was carrying a deadly weapon.

There were also many strange looking demons that were holding a rather large blade. When the people who are in terrible pain show resistance by shouting and attempting to climb out, these demons have the job of repeatedly stabbing the people with the blade, crushing their bodies, and throwing them back into the fire.

* Human Kabobs In Hell Resembling Chicken Kabobs

Jesus led me to another location where I almost fainted at what I witnessed. On my way home from school I often enjoyed buying skewered, boiled quail eggs and chicken kabobs to eat at the store. But, when I saw an image that resembled this chicken kabob in hell, I was shivering with shocked terror. It was a sight so terrifying and chilling that I didn't notice Jesus standing beside me.

A male, then a female, then another male and in that orderly fashion they were piled up high, and were not scattered even a bit, maybe because the giant demons were holding them from the side. All the people were naked and were stacked up into many levels. Some piles were about 130 ft tall, some were 328 ft tall, and still some were 492 ft tall.

Terror in the people was so vivid, and it seemed they had no way of resisting what was happening. When the human pile was ready, the demons took a long and sharp corkscrew-like instrument, which was much longer than the human pile, and pierced it through the chest. Soon the corkscrew had penetrated through the last person's chest at the bottom of the human pile. At that moment the simultaneous, agonizing screams sounded as though they would tear though the sky: "Ahhh! Please, help me! Please, please! Stop!"

The gigantic demons fixed the humans in place, and took another long corkscrew, and this time, pierced the lower abdomen area, and then held the human kabob up at once. The people continued to cry out, pleading for mercy. Some other demons approached, grinning, each holding a long skewer and began to stab and poke the people. "Save me! Please, stop doing this! Stop, just stop it! You damn demons!" and the people poured out curses — but it was no use. The blood began pouring out from the people. It looked similar to when my mother was boiling sweet potatoes. She would use a metal chopstick to poke them to see if they were fully cooked.

What was puzzling was that even though people were struggling with all their might, kicking and screaming, they did not fall. The demons were so gigantic they almost touched the sky, and their hair was curly, and the eyebrows and lashes were squirming like disgusting worms. "Yuk! This is horrible. Oh, it's hideous!" I involuntarily expressed my total disgust. The demons continued to shout and laugh out loudly, "Wow! This is great. It is really great" and they screamed out over and over again.

The long corkscrew the demon stabbed the pile of people with had a large handle, and the other demons came and lifted people up toward the blazing fire. Then they put them into the flaming fire and began to spin then around. At that moment the people on the corkscrew began to scream even louder in pain. "Ahhhh, save me! The pain is killing me. Ouch, it's so hot!" The demons cared less about the agonizing screams of the people and continued to cook them alive in the fire. The humans were getting the taste of both the pain inflicted by the kabob skewer as well as being cook alive simultaneously.

I questioned Jesus: "Jesus, how can they feel all these horrible pains? I am so terrified," and then the Lord replied, "Joo-Eun! No matter what painful punishments are inflicted on the people here in hell, all their senses are still alive — as it is for the people living on earth. Let's listen to what the demons are saying right now."

The demons took the grilled humans on the skewer off the fire and said, "It looks delicious. Which one of these fools should I eat first, in order or from the middle?" The grilled humans were not dead; instead they were scorched black and still alive but completely exhausted.

Each demon took a skewer saying, "Oh, never mind. I will eat them in order!" and then began tearing the flesh off like barbecue meat they crunched like they were munching on cartilage and bones. The crunching sound, each time the demon chewed the crushed bones of the people, rolled inside the demon's mouth. People screamed in pain and soon they disappeared from the demon's mouth.

The next person on the skewer waited, frightened and began to kick and scream, but there was no use. All of them were scorched black and shook violently in terror. One by one I witnessed the people being eaten alive by the demons, and I was filled with sadness and tears ran down my face. "Jesus, Jesus! I feel so sorry for these people. What do I do? I cannot bear to see them any more," and I sobbed.

Those scorched in the fire and eaten by the demons began to regenerate their flesh and bones. Then they were led in groups and some individually by various demons to be transferred to other parts of hell. The demons did not tell them where they were being taken, but when one suffering ended, without consideration they were all relocated to yet another place.

People shouted, "Where are you taking us now? Please, leave us alone. Have mercy, won't you?" and when they asked, the demons replied, "Shut up you fools! Can't you just shut your mouths and just follow?" and they began to stab them with a bluish sickle and severely beat them. It was then when Jesus led me to another location.

* A Huge Pile Of Torturing Tools

"Jesus! Where are you taking me right now?" When I asked the Lord, He answered and said I would know when I got there and was taken once again to where the head demon, Satan, was. Satan was sitting on his throne. But, there was something peculiar, because on the large table set before Satan there were countless amounts of horrible, sharp and scary tools and weapons piled up on it. Then an endless parade of people came in. There were just massive numbers of people; I don't have any sense of proportion as to how many people there were.

Upon closer look at the tools on the table, there were many tools that I recognized because we can see them daily on earth. There were shiny blue sickles, axes, many different blades of various sizes, hooks that were larger than human, whips, razor sharp forks, hoes, screwdrivers, augers, drills, spears, firearms, and many tools that can be used to beat and stab. The faces of the people in line turned pale thinking about what lay ahead.

While Jesus and I were watching the king demon, Satan, in a large pit, Jesus said "Let us go in a little farther," and He pulled me by the hand. One side of me was scared, but I felt safe because Jesus was by my side. Before long we reached where the king demon was and around Satan and his followers we began to see many souls more closely.

* Joo-Eun Faces Satan Again

In hell, Satan poured out curses at the souls while preparing to torture them. Our eyes met. When our eyes met, he gave me the scary stare down and suddenly yelled out loudly.

"You! Why are you here again? Leave now! Why, why again? Huh, why do you keep coming here! Are you trying to gouge my eyes out and tear my wings again like last time? Hey! There are no wings this time. I didn't make them. Hey you piggy! Hey you son of a bitch! Why are you continuously bothering me?" There were curses I dare not repeat which he kept spewing out at me. The king demon definitely brewed deep anger towards me, but he was on his guard against me because he was afraid I would use Jesus" authority to retaliate.

Satan didn't see me as a young minor; instead he cursed at me without ceasing like when the ignorant and unreasonably angry adults engage in an out-of-control fight. All the while he was being cautious of Jesus's expression, he began to speak again but without cursing, because he was scared of Jesus who was standing beside me, and he shouted at the top on his lungs "Ahhhh, man, ahhhh, man!" In that moment Jesus gave him a firm stare, and Satan became timid and hung his head low, falling forward, unable to speak, and then fell flat on his face.

I didn't want to miss this opportunity and shouted back at the king demon. "Hey! You damn, Satan! You want a piece of me? Damn you!" When I responded without fear Jesus burst loudly into laughter. As I did before, I wanted to climb on Satan and with regard I wanted to tear him apart, but Jesus persuaded me, "Joo-Eun! That's enough." He continued "My dear Sesame! If you continually provoke these filthy demons, they will disguise themselves and attack you and cause you great pain, so this time let it go."

After this the king demon continued on with spitting out unthinkable curses at me, and I can honestly say that I've never been cursed this much in my life. I was so furious, and to retaliate I began to curse him out, but I realized I didn't want to fill my mouth with such filth, so I stopped. Then I pleaded with Jesus: "Jesus! That filthy Satan is cursing at me too much. I am so angry and it's killing me inside." And just then Jesus commanded loudly, "Who do you think you are cursing at right now? You're a mere filthy demon and you dare to curse at my child, Joo-Eun?" At that Satan responded with trembling voice and vowed, "Yes, of course. I will not do it any more. I am sorry. I will never do it again."

I was so elated I began another round of attacks on Satan with bombarding him with abusive slander. Satan stared down at me helplessly, but the stare was communicating that he would avenge me later. He then repeated in a small voice, "You are dead. I will get you later!" While cautioned from Jesus's expressions, I provoked Satan by sticking out my tongue, saying, "Aren't you so mad? Ha-ha!" and I continued taunting him. The demon was about to explode with anger. I said to Jesus, "Jesus! I think I want to go now, because I don't want to see that filthy face of his!" Then the king demon, filled with irritation, ferociously said, "Shit, what did you say?"

Jesus said to me, "Joo-Eun, hell is where you will suffer for eternity. Also, all the souls in hell are here because they refused to accept me on earth — and it's an unforgivable sin. I want to forgive them, but they've already forfeited that chance. They are sinners, therefore, they have to endure and suffer whatever the punishments are for eternity. In hell some punishments are fixed for an individual, and for some it's not so, but regardless, each will suffer various calamities and live eternally within this curse." Afterwards Jesus wanted to take me to another location, so I followed Him.

* Room With Poisonous Insects

Jesus and I entered a room filled with all different crawling, poisonous insects when suddenly I realized I was trapped there alone. "Lord, Lord! Where are you?" and no matter how much I called, the Lord wasn't there. I now understand how sister Baek, Bong-Nyo felt. This appalling, disgusting and chilling scenario became a reality I had to deal with. I was trapped in a small, dark room and the dense, humid air pierced through my nostrils. Moments later strange insects swarmed around me, and I was unaware of where they came from.

There were bugs that looked like pine caterpillar, larvae, worms, centipedes, and many other species I'm not familiar with, and they began crawling up on me. I thought I was going to faint and I yelled desperately, "Yuck! Lord, where are you? Hey you disgusting bugs! Fire of the Holy Spirit! With the fire of the Holy Spirit burn them away!" and I pulled the bugs off of me. Thereupon the fire of the Holy Spirit came out of my body and in an instant incinerated all the bugs crawling on my body.

But, the insects on the floor continued to crawl up to my body. "Jesus, Jesus! Please save me! Where are you?" and I called out for Jesus, but He still was nowhere to be seen. "Oh, Jesus! Why did you bring to this place?" I cried and yelled. Finally Jesus appeared and took my hand and guided me back to church.

Jesus asked me how I was doing, and I replied that I never wanted to return to that room again. After my reply the Lord responded, "You will be all right! You are a child with a strong faith, therefore you can endure anything. I will use you mightily." The Lord promised to take me back to hell more often, because it is the best way to unlock the gift of spiritual sight and be certain of discernment, and through the visits to hell, things will soon become clearer.

February 11th, 2005 (Friday)

Sermon scripture: "I have written unto you, fathers, because ye have known him that is from the beginning. I have written unto you, young men, because ye are strong, and the word of God abideth in you, and ye have overcome the wicked one. Love not the world, neither the things that are in the world. If any man love the world, the love of the Father is not in him. For all that is in the world, the lust of the flesh, and the lust of the eyes, and the pride of life, is not of the Father, but is of the world." (1 John 2:14-16)

* A Military Demon Enters Sister Baek, Bong-Nyo

Pastor Kim, Yong-Doo: During the all night prayer vigil, for a split moment sister Baek, Bong-Nyo seemed absent-minded, and at that moment the demons entered into her like a swarm of bees. After praising for about three hours, and delivering the sermon, I had to be excused to use the restroom, and when I returned, I could see the demons continuing to enter into sister Baek, Bong-Nyo. She was rolling on the floor complaining of severe pain, and I could not stand watching her like this. I gathered the prayer team for emergency prayer and we urgently began praying as if our lives depending on it.

Why? I had an idea why the demons entered into sister Baek, Bong-Nyo, but I did not know for certain what the reasons were. It started in the evening. We were fighting desperately to cast out the demons until the next morning. Even with my powerful spiritual capabilities, along with my physical strength, I was gradually beginning to get fatigued, and the other members of the prayer team were out of energy, and one by one began collapsing to the side in exhaustion.

As He's done before, Jesus stood by without saying a word and very silently He observed us. To us, we are constantly in a hurry and urgently request His help and need solutions, but as Jesus was in control, He made sure that we endured each steps from the beginning. When I observed through my spiritual eyes, it was confirmed that this was the process.

All through the night we cried out and continued the spiritual battle of chasing out the demons — as well as being chased by the demons. We were in attack and retreat mode, and while we were engaged in the offensive and defensive battle, Jesus was always in observation, deeply in thought. Jesus was weighing our faith, and He wanted us to do the work ourselves with faith. But, when we've reached our limitations in a situation, He personally stepped in and intervened. Just as I assumed, Jesus was testing our limitations. I found out later that Jesus was allowing two angels to drive out the demons after a designated time.

When faced with the demons, what were the defensive and offensive battle plans Pastor Kim and the members of the Lord's Church utilized, and also, when the physical and spiritual strength were exhausted, what would happen if you fight until the end, in faith, without giving up….? The Lord holds very high expectations of us; therefore, we must try to work hard to sufficiently fulfill the Lord's high expectations at all time.

In a spiritual battle especially, the only plan of attack and victory can be obtained through prayer and trust in Jesus. There is no other way. In addition, our humanistic, temporary thoughts of rest or retreating from the battle strategy can not enter our minds. When we thought about it, our Lord's Church family members were all madly involved in our prayer and we looked quite crazy.

The evil demons that entered inside sister Baek, Bong-Nyo's body were exorcised out all night long, and we barely chased them out one by one. I must have shouted, "In the name of Jesus!" and "The fire of the Holy Spirit!" thousands of times. The demonic forces resisted until the end, even though they were burning from the fire of the Holy Spirit, but in the end only ashes remained.

So I thought, 'since they're all incinerated by the fire and turned into ash, it is finished.' Something totally unexpected and incomprehensible happened. The ashes restored back to life and transformed into a different demon. We did not succeed in retrieving the ashes out far enough and with our focus still on a victorious outcome, the situation turned for the worse.

This happened countless times. Therefore, even though the demonic forces inside are incinerated into ashes by the fire of the Holy Spirit, we must pull out all of the ashes completely to have the assurance. The sounds of the demons as they were cast out were very much similar to the sounds from the movie "The Exorcist" so I recorded the sound as evidence to properly document it.

* The Lord Snips The Demons With A Large Scissor

The amount of demonic forces that went inside sister Baek, Bong-Nyo surpassed anything I could have imagined. It was something that we could not fathom with our mind. Every one of us fell on the floor in complete exhaustion, and I dared to be a little annoyed at Jesus. The demons were spread out all over sister Baek's body like stretched-out rubber bands. "Jesus! Won"t you please help us! We can't do this any longer! What kinds of demons are these, so stubbornly strong and adhesive that we can't peel them off of the body? Oh Lord, please help us out of this situation! What time is it anyway?" I complained to Jesus, demanding that He help us, and after a long while Jesus finally intervened — because I guess looked pretty helpless.

Jesus was holding a very sharp scissor in one hand, and with that scissor He began to mercilessly snip off the demons that were covering sister Baek's body like rubber bands. At that moment, the demonic spirits cried out, begging for mercy and transformed into ashes, and then they became a smoke and disappeared.

With a stern expression, Jesus began rebuking us. "You must finish the fight with your faith to the end, but why did your faith become so weakened? When you pray in faith, there's nothing that you can't do. Why are you so afraid of the demons?" We gathered our bodies and minds together to regroup and sincerely repented before Jesus. Then after Jesus received all our prayers, He made a request saying, "Let's dance and celebrate joyfully for me." so we got up from where we were and danced with all our hearts.

Jesus then changed the atmosphere and calmed us down, and He spoke with sentiment and a warm voice. "To the sheep who love the Lord's Church: from now on when the demons and their forces of evil enter your body, do not be afraid! Instead defeat them with power and authority because nothing is impossible with faith, so be bold and strong!" Jesus desired us to attain victory and endure the fight with faith — no matter how hard it is — without expressing sadness or defeat. Instead, He wanted us to be joyful and victorious.

Our God the trinity has personally created us, and He utilizes each of our uniqueness to its fullness. Despite the situation, a child is without care or shame about their reputation or their outward appearances; likewise, we as a congregation dance and have fun during the service. Jesus desires us to be pure like little children.

Many believers today are aware of such truth, but in reality their attitude during the service is very different from the kind of service Jesus wants. There are areas where we need to be pure like a child, but also mature like an adult. "And said, Verily I say unto you, except ye be converted, and become as little children, ye shall not enter into the kingdom of heaven" (Matthew 18:3). "When I was a child, I talked like a child; I thought like a child, I reasoned like a child. When I became a man, I put childish ways behind me" (1

Corinthians 13:11) KJV.

The Lord is not someone who answers our prayers the moment we want, no matter when or what it is. Even when the demons enter into our bodies without warning, Jesus did not immediately resolve the problem; instead, He trained us to fight the demons with our faith. The Lord allowed any situations that will nurture our faith to mature.

* The Spiritual Lion Of Hell

Sister Baek, Bong-Nyo: As soon as I arrived at church the demons charged into my body while my mind was distracted. When Pastor Kim went to the restroom and came back after the sermon, in the blink of an eye the demons entered through my arms and legs. Without realizing, I let my guard down and became distracted, and it resulted in a serious mistake. I shouted inside to myself, 'Oh no, Lord! Once again today, the pastor and the congregation will not be able to pray because of me. What should I do?'

Pastor Kim, especially, used all his strength to chase the demons out of me, and it is not just one or two days, but these days he was driving out the demons daily. I am feeling so bad, and I don't know how to express my appreciation for him. I never imagined how difficult of a process it was to unlock the spiritual sight, and it was horrible dealing with the interference and attacks by the demons. When I began receiving one, two and more spiritual gifts, I turned pale, filled with surprised. The demons that pastor began driving out one by one looked disgusting to me. Those filthy demons spread all over my body, then lumped together into a conglomerated mass which inflicted a horrific physical pain, and they repeated this process.

I could no longer tolerate the pain on my back, and soon resorted to rolling on the church floor. I could see clearly the demons that were inside me, and those bastards were laughing, and they repeatedly transformed themselves into various images. In the midst of the craziness, one peculiarly strange looking spiritual lion from hell, wearing a black Korean traditional overcoat and a cylindrical Korean hat (made of bamboo or horsehair), appeared before me. I was terrified with fear and had goose bumps all over my body.

This filthy demon stared intently at me with its face as pale as a white piece of paper and began to speak. In its hands was a portrait of me and in a forceful, threatening voice said, "You! I am going to drag you to hell tonight, so here I am. I will finish you up tonight, so you might as well give up." This pest was determined to take me to hell, and stuck by my side, and no matter how much I prayed, I couldn't shake it off from me. At that moment I thought to myself, 'Oh! This lion from hell comes for those who are in their death bed and don"t believe in Jesus Christ.' I can't understand what people would think of the reality of what exists in the spiritual realm.

I, in turn, with the power of the Holy Spirit given to me by Jesus shouted, "Hey, you filthy demons! I command you in the name of God the trinity to fall back into the pit of hell where you came from!" and I grabbed this pestering demon by its throat and threw it far away from me.

February 14th, 2005 (Monday)

Sermon Scripture: "Surely the Lord GOD will do nothing, but he revealeth his secret unto his servants the prophets. The lion hath roared, who will not fear? the Lord GOD hath spoken, who can but prophesy?" (Amos 3:7-8) KJV

* Joseph Finally Receives His Gift Of Spiritual Sight

Joseph Kim: I just began praying at church when I noticed the stars in the night sky and the universe before my eyes, and I was in the midst of endless, open space of the galaxy. The spiritual realm that I've been hearing about was now clearly visible to me, and I can see that I was still on my knees and praying in tongues without falling down.

My physical body which was in prayer also felt the spiritual realm, and my soul was definitely experiencing every sensation as I was being absorbed into the spiritual world. Even as I was entering the spiritual realm, when I looked back, I could clearly see the church congregation in prayer.

* Angels And Their Wings

For the first time in my entire life I was seeing the angels ever so clearly, and it really was amazing and surreal. Pastor's body was standing behind the altar praying continually in tongues, and on the left side of the altar an angel with three sets of wings stood firmly. The wings were triangular and the length was quite long. I also saw other angels vaguely.

Also, the angel standing on the right side of the pastor was holding a golden bowl, and with that bowl the angel gathered up pastor's prayer like collecting falling rain. "And another angel came and stood at the altar, having a golden censer; and there was given unto him much incense, that he should offer it with the prayers of all saints upon the golden altar which was before the throne. And the smoke of the incense, which came with the prayers of the saints, ascended up before God out of the angel's hand" (Revelation 8:3-4) KJV.

* The Galaxy

I turned back and resumed going farther and deeper into the galaxy as if I was traveling in a time machine. As I traveled deeper I felt an amazing surge of speed. The countless stars in the galaxy passed by my right and left with a "swoosh!" sound, and with the loud swooshing noise, many stars began to move, giving an illusion that they were coming toward me to encircle me.

Initially I thought there were only dark skies and stars in the galaxy, but as I traveled farther, the color of the sky turned pale blue, and soon it became a glittering, shiny, brilliant rainbow of colors. The light from the rainbow was magnificent, like a fantasy.

February 15th, 2005 (Tuesday)

Sermon scripture: "Behold, I will do a new thing; now it shall spring forth; shall ye not know it? I will even make a way in the wilderness, and rivers in the desert. The beast of the field shall honour me, the dragons and the owls: because I give waters in the wilderness, and rivers in the desert, to give drink to my people, my chosen. This people have I formed for myself; they shall shew forth my praise." (Isaiah 43:19-21) KJV.

* Entering Through The Twelve Pearly Gates

Joseph Kim: Pastor suggested first that we pray. We decided to do the sermon after prayer; since it was just our family, he wanted to do things a little easy and free from structure. I agreed and I shouted with excitement, "Yes, I would like that. Let's begin with prayer first." Yesterday, near the end, my prayer was interrupted prematurely and I felt unsatisfied as if I missed out. I began praying filled with determination to enter into heaven again.

Only the pastor was up behind the altar praying, while mom, Joo-Eun and I knelt under the altar, each concentrating on praying. As soon as I cried out with a sincere prayer in tongues, just as yesterday, my spiritual sight opened up, and from a distance I saw heaven shinning brightly toward me. The closer I drew to the brilliant light, my heart pounded so hard, and I was filled with anticipation. I didn't know why my heart and body were trembling uncontrollably.

Finally, I was standing before the twelve pearly gates of heaven. There was an enormously large, round door, and on each side there were tall angels guarding the door. Those angels greeted me like they knew who I was saying, "Welcome, brother! Brother, you need an admission ticket to enter through here. I would like to see your ticket please!" and at that moment, not knowing how, in my hand was a small card, and I was shocked.

* The Admission Ticket Of Heaven And Its Description

I don't know when, who or how this beautiful card which represents heaven"s admission ticket got there, but regardless, the card was clearly in my hand. I proudly showed this card to the angels.

The exterior circumference of the admission ticket was adorned with gold, diamonds and jewels. In the middle was a cross stained with crimson blood, and it was sticky as if it was just stained moments ago. Right below, in an empty space, the symbol Alpha and Omega was engraved in the Hellenistic word, and my name was written in the heavenly word. Also, in the empty space above the cross was a drawing of two angels, face to face, and the back of the ticket was covered with gold and the words "Jesus Christ" distinctively written on it.

Jesus explained that normally the ticket to heaven is not visible, and only when you get to heaven's gate to enter will the ticket appear in your hand. Through Jesus's grace I was able to experience a unique spectacle in front of the heaven"s gate. Jesus said, "My dear, Piggy! We will go through the gates soon and you will not miss a thing, but right now pay close attention for just a moment to something special that is about to unfold before your eyes." So, Jesus and I stood in front of heaven's gate waiting.

There stood a soul before me whom I had compassion for because he looked so pathetic.
I wanted to reach out and lend him a helping hand, but Jesus said, "Wait, and just observe," so I did nothing but just observe. This individual was completely exhausted and could barely utter out a word because he was out of breath. "Oh my goodness, I have finally reached heaven's gate. Whew, I am all right now." As soon

as he finished his statement, the enormous angel who is the guardian of the pearly gates of heaven gave him a fierce stare and shouted. "Hey, you! Who are you and how dare you stand before the gates of heaven? You better get out of here right now!" The angel's demeanor was stern and full of dignity but also frightful.

This individual was wearing a dark garment and began to speak: "Please, angel, sir! This is the gate of heaven, right? You don't understand how hard it was to finally get here, so please! I have to enter through the gate. Won't you please have mercy on me, please?" and the angel responded. "Is that so? Then let me see your admission ticket!" "Huh? What admission ticket? What should I do, because I don't have anything like that?" Then the angel replied, "I thought so! How dare you come here without an admission ticket and act frivolously! Get out of my sight!" With that said, the angel hit the individual with his fingers as if playing with a marble. With a scream, the person flew at a speed faster than a missile and fell into hell. This individual fell precisely into the middle of the fiery pit of hell and soon cried out for mercy.

As I watched all that was happening, Jesus spoke to me: "Joseph! Do you understand now? You can never enter through the heavenly gate if you do not have the ticket. You too must be alert and live faithfully. Do you understand?" I answered, "Yes, Jesus! I understand very clearly." The angels's expressions returned back from terror to gentleness and warmth, and they bowed their heads.

Jesus said, "All right, let's enter through the gate. It's getting late," so I followed behind Jesus. It looked as though the round pearl was slightly rolling, when suddenly I realized I was already inside the illuminated world. My eyes and mouth fell to the floor in awe and I especially could not close my mouth. "Wow! This is marvelous! Wow!" I was suddenly standing before a gigantic . . . someone.

* Joseph Sees The Throne Of God

A gigantic . . . giant? . . . was wearing a garment that was whiter than the snow. He was sitting on the throne. There were rainbows surrounding and shinning all around, and there are no words to describe what I was seeing. Also, the area above the chest was covered by fog-like clouds. As soon as I tried to lift my head up, it automatically bowed down, and the majesty, glory and light weighed down on me.

I thought inside, 'This is Jehovah God!' and I lifted my head up to see. God's figuration was like us humans, and He reached the top of the sky sitting down. He was tremendously big and seemed unfathomable.

"And immediately I was in the spirit: and, behold, a throne was set in heaven, and one sat on the throne. And he that sat was to look upon like a jasper and a sardine stone: and there was a rainbow round about the throne, in sight like unto an emerald" (Revelation 4:2-3) KJV.

An intense light poured out from God the Father's facial area, and my head automatically bowed down once again. God spoke with a strong, thundering voice, "Oh, Joseph, my little pig has come. You went through a lot to get here. I will give you mighty abilities, so continue praying diligently!" As soon as I heard our Father God's voice, my body froze in place like I was just hit with an electric shock, and I could not move at all.

After that, I followed Jesus to travel around heaven, visiting many places that were like the Garden of Eden. It was an amazing place. There were columns of unknown jewels I've never seen before and the lights reflected off them shined even brighter. I can see the Archangel Michael riding on a white horse at a distance.

* Joseph Receives A Scroll

That day we started with prayer first and then later pastor followed with praising and a sermon. While I was worshipping, I could see clearly the throne of God. I could see it with my eyes closed as well as opened. I saw an enormously large scroll and God the Father was holding one side with His mighty hand. Suddenly the other side of the scroll began to unroll and rolled and rolled until it reached where I was worshipping. I stretched both my arms out as far as I could and respectfully accepted the scroll. The magnitude of its weight was felt right away.

When I observed the scroll with my eyes, I could not recognize, let alone understand because it was written in a foreign, heavenly language, and to me it looked like a hieroglyphic or a cuneiform. It was mind-boggling to stare at the scroll filled and recorded with small and large heavenly writings. The scroll did not end, but was connected from heaven, and at that moment

God the Father spoke in my ears resoundingly clearly. "Joseph! You will become an especially great pastor, and this is my gift to you!" I jumped up and down from where I was sitting.

God the Father continued to promise in a deep, resounding voice to pour out mighty powers and many abilities upon me. My father, who was also a pastor, seemed to look upon me with an enormous envy. For some time I was enduring hardship because I did not receive the spiritual gift of sight. When the other members of the congregation were receiving the gift of spiritual sight as well as various other spiritual gifts, I felt alone and hurt inside, but finally the dream of receiving the gift to awaken my spiritual sight was becoming a reality for me. I didn't know how to show my gratitude to my God the Trinity. I resumed praying in tongues and I was immediately taken before the throne of God. I felt even more insignificant than a speck of dust before God's presence. God reminded me again that I have a calling to be a pastor in the future, and He gave me another special gift, and it was a treasure box.

Then, while I was still at the throne of God, I saw precisely four beasts: one was a lion, a calf, a beast with the face of a human, and an eagle soaring with its wings — just as it is mentioned in the book of Revelation 4:7. There were six wings attached to it, with countless eyes in the front as well as the back, and it looked closely and observed what was happening on earth where we lived. As the angels opened up the book of life before the throne of God, God turned the pages of the book one by one looking for something.

* A Bottle Filled With Tears

A short while later God"s enormous hand found and confirmed the matter He had in mind from the book of life. So, after He found it, He pointed at me saying, "Joseph Kim!" and then commanded, "Bring me Joseph's bottle for his tears, as well as sister Shin, Sung-Kyung's tear bottle to me."

"Thou tellest my wanderings: put thou my tears into thy bottle: are they not in thy book?" (Psalm 56:8) KJV.

Immediately after the command was given, in a blink of an eye, an angel brought the bottles, but some were big and some were small. I didn't know the reason why God asked for deaconess Shin and my tear bottle, but lately she's been crying often while she prayed, so I think God wanted me to verify it with my eyes.

After seeing the tear bottles, I was able to enjoy sightseeing many of the houses in heaven, but you can't help but to be in awe of its enormous size and plan. Like bamboo sprouts after a rainfall, the houses were sprung out everywhere and they were various shapes and sizes. Also, God gave me a crown for my head, and it was a brilliantly shining crown that fit perfectly on my head. As soon as I receive this crown on my head, an overwhelming joy flowed inside me and I ran all over to continue sightseeing.

Chapter 2
Holy Spirit's Poisonous Thorn

February 17th, 2005 (Thursday)

Sermon Scripture: "For the earth bringeth forth fruit of herself; first the blade, then the ear, after that the full corn in the ear. But when the fruit is brought forth, immediately he putteth in the sickle, because the harvest is come." (Mark 4:28-29) KJV.

* Falling Asleep In The Arms Of Jesus

Kim, Joo-Eun: While I was praying, Jesus came and stood before me. "Jesus, Jesus! I finally graduated from elementary school today. Jesus, as my graduation present, please take me to visit heaven," and to my request the Lord replied: "Really? When you pray diligently I will certainly take you to heaven. So pray without ceasing." I began to call out to the Lord in prayer, and He applauded me by saying, "My Sesame, you are praying especially hard today. Oh, you are doing well!"

I began to repent to Jesus for all the sins I committed, and I cried out to Him until I was completely exhausted. At that moment Jesus sat in front of me and said, "Sesame! Are you tired? Come to me" and then He embraced me. He laid my head gently down on His knee and said "Sesame! Since you are so exhausted today, let's postpone your visit to heaven for next time; instead, rest in my arms" and He began tapping me on my back. I asked Jesus, "Jesus! If I fall asleep while praying the demons will attack me. Do you think I will be ok?" The Lord replied,
"I will protect you, so do not worry. Now, my dear Sesame, go to sleep. Go to sleep…"

I fell into a deep sleep in Jesus's warm embrace.

* The Demon From The Movie "The Ghost Of A High School"

Joseph Kim: While the music was playing the praise song

"Receive the Holy Spirit" my body became a ball of fire, and when the music gradually slowed down to a mellow praise song, my prayer also became lax. I felt that I was standing in a dark hallway of a school like in the movie "The Ghost of a High School." Suddenly, from a far, dark corner, a demon wearing a white gown stood still with her long hair waving in the wind. Upon seeing the demon, a cold chill spread all over my body, and immediately it began charging at me in a zig zagging motion with a loud noise: "Bang, bang, bang, and bang," and then she pinned me down. The female demon's face was covered with her long hair, and I was absolutely terrified and thought I was going to faint, but I tried real hard not to express my fear on my face. The demon shoved her face right at the tip of my nose, and she opened her Dracula-like mouth with her sharp fangs protruding out, and with her eyes and mouth bleeding, she came toward me to intimidate me. I shouted out, "In the name of Jesus flee from me! You filthy demon!" and just then the demon screeched and vanished.

I continued to pray when the throne of God began to appear before my eyes, and it looked like God was preparing to give me something. I thought, 'What will He give me this time?' and I was filled with curiosity, so I concentrated on praying more diligently.

* Massive Scrolls Descending From Heaven

I could see countless scrolls in a large pile as tall as a mountain before the throne of God, and among them the largest scroll rolled round and round, descending toward where I was. The thickness of the scroll was approximately 3 feet and about 6 feet wide, and it looked quite large and heavy. I didn't know how I was going to catch this scroll that was approaching me at an enormous speed. The four beasts in front of God's throne observed carefully with their eyes fixated on what was happening.

At last, I stretched out my arms to receive this large scroll, but never mind how large it was, I barely caught it because it was so heavy that I almost fell back. The scroll was white, but glittering with gold, and it naturally entered into my body. The writing on it looked similar to Hebrew. While I was praising and listening to the sermon, countless scrolls of all sizes descended down continuously toward me. Later on the scrolls overlapped into a large pile, so I didn't know what to do at times. The scrolls entered into my head, chest, mouth as well as my hands. "Wow! Oh my! What is happening?" and I was talking out loud without knowing it. "Pastor! Pastor! There are countless scrolls descending from the throne of God down into my body right now!"

When the pastor heard my voice, he came toward me and with a childlike curiosity said, "Really? Hey! Don't just receive them all for yourself — share them with me." He then stood directly in front of me and began receiving the scrolls that were intended for me. But strangely, the scrolls reflected off of pastor and every single one of them entered into my body. I said "Pastor! It doesn't matter that you are standing in front of me. These scrolls are given to me by God." and I laughed but pastor expressed disappointment.

At that moment Jesus said, "Pastor Kim has already received them all."

* Grandmother Imprisoned In A Glass Bottle In Hell

Lee, Yoo-Kyung: Only the pastor and his family were at church having their own service and praying, but I a strong desire to go and pray. So, I went to church to worship and while I was praying, Jesus came to me and suddenly took me to hell.

Jesus led me to a place with many glass bottles, and inside were many people who were running around. I could hear them screaming out for help. Below the bottles were red hot flames and soon the bottles were bright red, and people in them looked crazy.

I heard a familiar voice among them that sounded like my

grandmother, and I thought I was going to faint. "Yoo-Kyung? Dear Yoo-Kyung! It's so hot here! Oh I am suffocating in here! Please save me. Won't you help your granny from this place! Hurry and ask Jesus for help, hurry!" My grandmother yelled at me from inside the bottle. I looked at her and replied "Grandma, grandma! What do I do? Oh my heart! You filthy demons! Why are you torturing my grandmother with fire? Grandma!" I pleaded with Jesus: "Jesus! Please, save my grandmother, won't you please?" and He said: "Yoo-Kyung! It is dangerous, so do not go too close to the bottle. Don't be too close. It is dangerous, even for you!" Jesus held my hands tightly so that I would not walk any closer toward the bottle.

No matter how much I begged, Jesus did not do what I asked, so I began to shout to God. "Father God! Oh my Father God! Please save my grandmother, please!" but God the Father did not say one word. My grandmother began to run around frantically as the bottle got hotter, and soon her feet melted onto the bottom of the bottle, gradually turning her black because she was dying. Her voice died down to a very low pitch. Suddenly she screamed out loud because the heat was so intense, and then she collapsed again. My grandmother ran around in circles until all of her legs were melted down and she looked completely out of her mind.

Beside the bottle was a horned demon guarding and saying, "Hahahaha! Today we have delicious meat to eat once again. I am so happy. Hahahhaha!" and it continued to laugh. That same demon stabbed with its horns the people lined up to get inside the bottle and they fell in with screaming cries.

The demon began licking the blood spattered onto its body saying, "Delicious, really delicious!" and continued to lick the blood off. The demons inflicted cuts and began to suck the blood out, and when the blood was gone they would slice more wounds, allowing more blood to pour out, and again proceeded to lick them off. It was such a horrific sight, and I didn't want to see it, but I could not hide from it. I continually sobbed because of my grandmother. I was engulfed in sorrow, so Jesus tried to comfort me saying, "Shsss, now, there, there!" and He tried to comfort me four times. "Yoo-Kyung! Come now and stop your crying. Stop crying!"

But the evil demons stood in front of the bottle and danced happily in front of the suffering people for them to see. Jesus said, "Yoo-Kyung! Let's go to heaven now," and so I followed Jesus to heaven and I left behind the horrible images of my grandmother's suffering and the painful screams. When I arrived in heaven, I ate until my heart's content all the various fruits Jesus gave me to eat and then retuned to church.

February 18th, 2005 (Friday)

Sermon Scripture: "The LORD hear thee in the day of trouble; the name of the God of Jacob defend thee; Send thee help from the sanctuary, and strengthen thee out of Zion; Remember all thy offerings, and accept thy burnt sacrifice; Selah" (Psalm 20:1-3) KJV.

Joseph Kim: As the worship began I started praising when suddenly my spiritual sight opened up, and at first God's throne was vaguely visible, but soon it became crystal clear. I heard a voice from the Father God saying, "You will be my servant and do my work; therefore, I will enable you to see clearly and always the spiritual realm with your eyes. Do not be arrogant, but be humble to the end."

Also, our heavenly Father had something in His mighty hand, and it was a gold crown with various jewels adorning it — which God himself put on my head. As soon as the gold crown was on my head I felt a flow of electricity, and because the crown was shining so brightly, I could not see it properly.

* The Descending Of The Full Armor Of God

An enormous brilliance was shining from the throne of God when the golden radiance of the sword of the Holy Spirit began to slowly descend down, and I instinctually thought to myself, 'Oh! This must be the sword of the Spirit that I've only heard about.' I remembered reading Ephesians 6 some time ago and desiring to receive the sword of the Spirit, so I earnestly prayed for it. And now that sword of the Spirit was descending toward me! The scene I imagined was happening right in front of my eyes.

If it was possible, I wanted to possess the full armor of God. "Put on the whole armour of God, that ye may be able to stand against the wiles of the devil" (Ephesians 6:11) KJV. The shinning gold sword of the Spirit continued to descend directly to me, and suddenly a thought said to me that I needed to swallow the sword, so I opened my mouth wide. The sword entered through my mouth and was situated in my stomach. Surprisingly, I didn't get sick nor was I struck with pain.

Something else began to descend, and it was a marvelous shield which looked like it was made of gold, and it was shinning so brightly as it also entered into my body. A few other swords of the spirit descended from above and once again I swallowed them up. I also saw the helmets the generals from our history wore in war. I thought, 'Oh! This must be the helmet of salvation. This helmet of salvation entered into my body.'

Following this, the shield of faith descended with various lights harmoniously shining from it — so many golden lights illuminating ever so brightly. This shield also entered into my body. The shoes to be fitted with the readiness that comes from gospel of peace were similar to boots made of gold, as well as the breastplate of righteousness and the belt of truth were made of gold.

A little while later a living object was running all about and it charged toward me, and I realized it was an enormously large white horse. Without any fear or hesitation, in an instant I jumped on the back of the charging white horse and the horse began to fly all over the sky. I felt such an absolute exhilaration, and I can't describe in words what that happiness felt like. While I was still flying on the white horse, something continuously descended from the throne of God to me. I saw a golden sack and the inside was filled with food and drinks. Also, a Chinese character slowly descended, and I stretched out my hands to grab it to post it securely on my chest.

"Above all, taking the shield of faith, wherewith ye shall be able to quench all the fiery darts of the wicked" (Ephesians 6:16) KJV

As mentioned, I was being prepared for the future, fiery battles with the demons. There were also many victory flags descending from heaven which entered into my body, as well as a map of the world that immediately went into my mouth. The trumpet, which signifies the good news of the Gospel, made of gold, also entered into my mouth.

Next, to attack the evil demons in the battle all kinds of weapons began descending from heaven, and there were swords and spears of every size, axes, double-edged swords, iron hammers, a commanding general's patch, awarding plaque, a three-pronged spear, scissors, air rifles, electrical shocking instruments, bow and arrow, a handheld fan, books, eagles, binoculars, missiles, cannons, a flame thrower, airplane, warships, stars, chairs, rainbows, spoons, chopsticks, marbles, and countless many others — ceaselessly descended down.

I wanted to know and confirm the reason with the heavenly Father why I was given all these weapons, and so I asked once more: "My heavenly Father! Why did you give me so many different weapons?"

At this God replied, "You will be traveling all over the world to save many lost souls. This is the reason why I am giving you these weapons. Also, in a short while you will be fighting the king demon, Satan, and when you battle the demons you will need such weapons, and I will give you more powerful weapons. You will receive the blazing fire of the Holy Spirit and electricity. But, if you become arrogant and corrupt I will withdraw all your abilities I've given you, and you will lose your gifts to someone else, so stay humble until the end and do not become arrogant! Do you understand?" I bowed down with respect before God the Father and I replied, "Yes, God." Additionally, God promised to pour down all the heavenly gifts that I will need in my ministry in the future as a pastor.

Shortly after, 12 angels from heaven descended with a carriage led by the white horse, and they proclaimed that the special gifts they brought were directly from God, and then the gifts entered into my body. These gifts represented God's words more than any other gifts I've received, and many, various sizes of the swords of the Spirit especially entered into my body this time.

Also, a rolled-up rug shining in a reddish shade descended down in front of me, but immediately when the rug spread open tons of jewels began to pour out of it. I felt like I was the main character in a story book. There was a valuable jewelry box that caught my eyes, so when I opened it, a blinding light streamed out and I thought I was going to faint.

All these things were so clearly visible to me, and I felt I was in a trance because what I saw was so beautiful, that I was about to loose my consciousness.

* Jesus's Warning About Sufferings We Will Endure In Hell

Sister Baek, Bong-Nyo: Jesus said, "To transform Pastor Kim, before anything, I will bring him to hell and for 3 1/2 years he will be imprisoned there, and he will experience the sufferings of hell first hand." Pastor Kim responded in shock: "No Lord, please no! You know that I am a coward inside! Unlike what my exterior portrays, I am tender, gentle inside, and easily frightened!" Just then Jesus burst into laughter, saying, "You are stronger than you think, and I know so." Pastor Kim and his family are very amusing sometimes. He never displays how tired he is; instead, when I witness the over-flowing happiness he exudes, I have been envious of him on more than one occasion.

Lately I've noticed that Jesus is a constant guest in the pastor's home. When I ask the Lord where He is, He often tells me He's at the pastor's house, and I only get to hear Him speaking to me.

* Pastor Kim's Supplication

Pastor's wife, Kang, Hyun-Ja: Jesus said to Pastor Kim, "You are a pastor, but you also have the responsibility of writing the books for the world to read; therefore, you must personally experience what hell is like. Also, this will allow you to pay close attention and realize the things you must correct, so from this time forward be solidly prepared and ready. You have to especially visit where my fallen servants end up, and you will suffer greatly from various places of hell, starting from the bottom." With that said, Pastor Kim was shaking violently in fear.

Jesus allowed us to realize and know why He delayed Pastor Kim and my gifts of spiritual sight, and it was because we had sinned by disclosing the secret.

Pastor Kim spoke in a defiant tone of voice saying, "Jesus! Please no. Why do I have to suffer the pain just because of the fact that I am a pastor? That's not fair. Jesus, if you really treat me that way, I will stop writing the book. I really don't want to go to hell!" and he shouted. Then Jesus replied with a firm voice, "Pastor Kim! Be strong. Why do you have so much fear?" and Jesus reassured him.

Joseph and Joo-Eun were listening beside me, and responded. "Dad! Are you really a pastor? Why are you saying all these weak things? Really……" When our kids gave their opinions, pastor's pride was hurt, and his face looked unhappy. Our Jesus expressed compassion and love and comforted him. "Pastor Kim! I will give you the strength, so don't worry yourself too much! I will lessen the pain you will have to suffer."

For the moment you will not see and your body's senses will only feel stinging, and He reassured that both pastor and I will experience similar sensations. Both of us were hugely relieved and let out a sigh.

* Jesus's Humanistic Nature

The Jesus we experienced displayed so much more humanity than what we expect, displaying warmth, and despite being a spirit, He is very sentimental. Even when we don't firmly hold the Bible to go witness, and each time we are encounter difficulties and suffer from exhaustion, He feels loving compassion for us and abundantly comforts us. As the son of God, He rules over all creation with authority, but each word He speaks to us melts our hearts. There is not even one person who would not be moved by such love that can be felt so deep inside. Jesus is very sensitive to emotions and His humanity overflows.

We often have the tendency to see Jesus only as a judge and know Him as a Holy Lord. This doesn't mean I am suggesting you regard our Holy Lord carelessly or lightly.

For the most of us, ordinary Christians or the church may not know, but Jesus has a very great sense of humor. Also, when we are upset and crying He will cry with us, and grieve with us, and when we are happy He rejoices with us. He is Holy, but I would like to express that our Lord is extremely jealous when He is replaced by our excessive preoccupation with the things of this world.

Therefore, our families live daily and are especially cautious so that we do not disappoint or hurt our Trinity God. When we are leading a conversation, we make sure that we do not leave out talks about our Heavenly Father, Jesus or the Holy Spirit. Jesus and the Holy Spirit — seeing our devotion — are always by our side and allow us to see them, and they pour down all the fire and energy upon our bodies. Additionally, after we received the gift of spiritual sight we began experiencing many surprising, shocking and unimaginable things on daily basis.

* Jesus's Humor

Our family was sitting around and sharing a conversation about heaven, and sharing our opinions about Jesus and the Holy Spirit when we realized the room was soon filled with Jesus, Holy Spirit and the angels enjoying our conversation.

Jesus seemed especially in the mood to joke around with my husband, Pastor Kim, and began to speak. "Pastor Kim! You are a pastor and have a great faith, therefore you must suffer great pain so that your spiritual sight will quickly open up — so what do you think? Are you ready to go right now?" Jesus asked Joo-Eun to deliver this question to him.

At this, my husband jumped up in shock, shouting, "Oh, Lord! You're going to start that again? Why do you keep scaring me?" and we all laughed at his response. Even though what Jesus was asking seemed like a joke, there was a hidden truth in what He was saying.

Jesus explained that there was a huge difference in simply visiting hell and actually experiencing hell, and the only way to write the books without compromising them was to feel the pain and personally experience the reality of the suffering. This way the only way the book's content would be authentic, and pastor Kim would be ready to be utilized mightily in the future. After this explanation pastor began to get terrified. The Lord continued, this time directly to me, "Since you are the wife of the pastor and are in the same boat, therefore, wouldn't it make sense that you also join him in experiencing hell?" I was so surprised I shouted, "Jesus! I am really someone who gets scared easily. I am especially terrified of hell. I am a weak servant and I will not last even one minute or one second." And just then Jesus burst into laughter, saying "Oh no, no — I don't think so! You are strong." Soon Pastor Kim was beside me laughing and delightfully agreeing with the Lord to tease me. "Hahahaha! Lord you are so right. Sister Kang, Hyun-Ja is much tougher than she looks. Just look at her forearms. Doesn't she look like she can cause some serious damage with them to those demons?"

I tried to use a childish voice and charm and pleaded, "Oh Jesus! This isn't right. Since I am so scared, I would like to just observe if I may, please?!" So Jesus replied, "Okay, okay, as you wish! I will allow you to observe only." I was shouting for joy.

So pastor sat beside me and with his small eyes he stared me down and said, "Hey, where is your loyalty? While your beloved husband is suffering in hell, all the years of love and loyalty should allow you to say, 'Honey! I will be right beside you, so don't worry! We will live and die together.' but what? You are so happy that you would not be suffering the pain in hell? Man… what can I say." and he chuckled.

"Pastor Kim! Don't worry. Jesus will be with you and protect you, so best of luck to you in hell!" and as soon as I said this, Jesus burst into a loud laughter, "Hahahaha!" The kids said in unison, "Dad! You are in big trouble!" and began to laugh.

Suddenly, it was apparent that pastor was terribly worried about what experiences he will endure in hell. Jesus went one step further and said, "From now on, Pastor Kim must thoroughly prepare your mind and go even deeper into prayer." Pastor asked a question: "Jesus! When I am imprisoned in hell and suffer much pain, would my reward in heaven become greater?" Jesus explained that the reasons for the suffering weren't for the reward, but to correctly write the books of that experience. The physical battle pastor had to endure while fighting with the demons was his portion of faith that he must complete. When it's done he will receive the reward.

Jesus encouraged Pastor Kim for the physical sufferings that he must experience in hell in the near future, and He showed Joo-Eun pastor's house in heaven. Joo-Eun reported that Pastor Kim's house was already 900 stories high and mine was up 700 stories and countless angels were busy in construction of the house.

* The Spiritual Cell Phone And The Text Messages

Pastor Kim pleaded, "Jesus! Please revive our church." and suddenly pastor's spiritual cell phone began to ring. Pastor Kim's spiritual cell phone had a spiritual text message from Jesus regarding the request, and it said simply going out to witness to people isn't easy, therefore, we must go out by equipping ourselves with much prayer and with the power given to us from above. The kids also verified this with their spiritual eyes. Jesus shouted out loudly that the Lord's Church will be revived and grow, therefore we must pray and evangelize diligently.

February 19th, 2005 (Saturday)

Sermon Scripture: "I indeed baptize you with water unto repentance. but he that cometh after me is mightier than I, whose shoes I am not worthy to bear: he shall baptize you with the Holy Ghost, and with fire: Whose fan is in his hand, and he will thoroughly purge his floor, and gather his wheat into the garner; but he will burn up the chaff with unquenchable fire." (Matthew 3:11-12) KJV

Kim, Joseph: When I close my eyes or am in prayer I can see the throne of God ever so clearly before me. Just a few days before I was frustrated when I heard the experiences of those with spiritual sight, because I did not yet receive the gift of the spiritual sight, and with envy and sadness I often sat alone in one corner of the church with tears in my eyes. Now I am able to see the throne of God engulfed in majestic brilliance before my eyes. It was much more blinding than the sunlight, ten thousands times brighter.

I tried hard to see the throne of God more clearly with my eyes, but each time I raised my head to look the illuminating brilliance and its majesty involuntarily bowed my head and I was unable to see it clearly. I could see a bit of the enormous knees and the feet. God is mighty and unfathomably gigantic. Before the throne of God the four beasts are there with their fierce stares, and they looked toward where I was and their eyes rolled all about (Revelation 4:6). Also, there were various lights shining from the throne and their hues were unclear, but they looked like uncommon shades of a rainbow.

* A Golden Road Connecting To Heaven

An unfamiliar, special golden light began appearing brightly before me, so I paid close attention to what was being revealed.

Without thinking, I shouted, "Wow, it's the road to heaven!" From where I was standing, I've never seen anything like the endless road leading up to heaven. Even those at church with their spiritual gift of sight have not seen this road leading to heaven, but God showed it to me clearly and precisely.

The width of the road wasn't very wide, but it leads directly to God"s throne, and the golden road began right under my nose. The golden lights continued to shine, and from a distance some object was coming toward my direction.

* The Heavenly Treasure Necessary In Ministry

Anything descending from heaven, no matter what it is, shines so brightly and when I try to look with my eyes I can hardly open my eyes due to the glare, and I'm guessing it will damage my vision. The objects I saw from a distance were still racing toward me, and the closer they approached, their identities were clearly revealed. There were three to four heavenly angels hauling the golden carriage, and at the head leading was a horse as white as snow as the angels held the halter like coachmen and led the carriage down.

Inside the golden carriage were many red, wrapping cloths, and I was anxious to see what was inside the cloths. As soon as they arrived, the angels brought the packages from the carriage and politely spoke. "Greetings, Brother Joseph! God commanded us to deliver these to you, hence we are here. Brother Joseph you will be involved in ministry as a pastor and God said that all the things necessary for you in your ministry are in here. Please utilize them appropriately."

I began to open each package one by one as the angels brought them to me, and inside, overflowing, were all kinds of jewels and precious treasures in unthinkable quantities, and each of them was brilliantly shinning. Even after the angels and the carriage ascended back to heaven the packages continued to pour down.

God unceasingly poured down on me.

I asked the heavenly Father: "Heavenly Father! Why are you giving me such priceless gifts? I don't know what to say." Jesus stood beside me and tenderly requested, "Joseph! You will stand before the whole world as the servant of the Lord and you will be used in a mighty way! Therefore, do not become arrogant, but be humble until the end. Do not be led astray and become corrupt. These are given so that you may do much more for my name so take them and use them wisely. You will be a prominent figure and will be a huge influence in the world!"

After that, many other packages containing unknown gifts continued to descend down to me. I began to open my mouth like I was eating food and swallowed all the gifts which then entered into my stomach one by one. When I saw myself with spiritual eyes, I was enormously bloated and fat because I swallowed so many things.

* Touched By Jesus

Sister Kang, Hyun-Ja: Today I was suddenly attacked by sadness, so I began to cry out in prayer, and as if a camera light was flashing, a light began flashing on and off a few times. I was suddenly surprised, so I decided to ask my daughter who was praying beside me.

A short while later I felt someone concentrating and continually touching me on my head, back and hands. Joseph and Joo-Eun sarcastically said, "Mom! Are you trying to tease someone? Right now Jesus is the one who's touching you. Don't you know that?" and they rebuked me.
So I decided to ask Jesus and the Lord told me not to worry and to continue praying.

* Haak-Sung Meets Moses

Lee, Haak-Sung: While I was praying Jesus came and took me to heaven, and I finally met Moses whom I've longed to meet. As soon as I met Moses I shouted at the top of my lungs: "Moses, sir! Moses sir! I wanted to meet you so much!" Moses replied, "Ah-ha, Brother Haak- Sung! It's nice to meet you." and he took my hand.

Moses continued: "Currently in heaven there is widespread talk about the Lord's Church. I especially wanted to meet Pastor Kim, Yong-Doo, but why isn't he here? Instead, why have you come to see me instead, Brother Lee?" I felt humiliated by his comment and didn't know what to do. Moses said that many famous, faithful servants from the Bible are waiting to meet Pastor Kim and I was asked to deliver this message to urge him to quickly receive the gift of spiritual sight, so they can meet in heaven.

At that moment, as Jesus was listening to this conversation, He suddenly spoke loudly saying, "I am the greatest one!" and both Moses and I instantly bowed our heads down.

I returned to church, and after I finished praying, I delivered what Moses said, and pastor said: "Haak-Sung! I am a pastor of a small start-up church and I am no one significant, so why would the great servants want to meet me? I can't understand that." At that moment Jesus stood beside me and once again repeated what He said in heaven: "I am greater than any prominent servants from the Bible!"

February 21st, 2005 (Monday)

Scripture sermon: "Beloved, think it not strange concerning the fiery trial which is to try you, as though some strange thing happened unto you: But rejoice, inasmuch as ye are partakers of Christ's sufferings; that, when his glory shall be revealed, ye may be glad also with exceeding joy." (1 Peter 4:12-13)

* Mrs. Kang, Hyun-Ja And Sister Baek, Bong-Nyu, Incursion From Evil Spirits

Pastor Kim, Yong Doo: My wife and Sister Baek, Bong-Nyu prayed for the gift of having their spiritual eyes opened. They began praying last night and had finished this morning at 9 a.m. The thought of going home must have slipped their minds; they continued to converse with one another. They had prayed all night. They should sleep and rest, but they did not appear exhausted. They just continued to converse with one another.

I advised them that the Lord will grant them opened spiritual eyes and with all other gifts at the proper time. I told them to cease speaking about the matter. The more one spoke, the greater the chance of vulnerability for evil spirits to attack. Therefore, I had advised them to stop and go home and rest. However, they continued to sit next to each other and converse uncontrollably. There was no sign of them stopping. I reluctantly left them and went home and slept. My wife came home after a long time. Then the accident occurred.

"Neither give place to the devil." (Ephesians 4:27)
"Let all things be done decently and in order." (1 Corinthians 14:40)
"..To obey is better than sacrifice, and to hearken than the fat of rams." (1 Samuel 15:22)

After Sister Baek, Bong-Nyu had left my wife, it was about noon when she headed home. About that time, as she was climbing down the stairs, an unidentified group of dark evil forces attacked her. They wrapped around her body and made her fall.

Initially, the evil spirits had waited and hovered around her. When they found a vulnerability, they quickly spun like a whirlwind tornado in great speed. They made her dizzy. Although she was very dizzy and had to sit on the stairs, she attempted to hold her ground, clenching her teeth. With their full strength, the evil spirits pushed her, and she rolled down to the end of the stairs. As a result, she broke her back and was taken to the hospital. She had to have an operation that fastened her back bone with steel. This accident was caused by disobedience and a bit of complacency.

Jesus did not personally heal her, but He had told her to get an operation. When we asked why the Lord would not heal her and instead go to the hospital, He said that depended on the faith of the person. Sometimes the Lord would personally heal people, but He also would use doctors for medical attention. Doctors are used by Him as a means to treat and heal people.

"Saint Bong-Nyu has some areas that need to be evaluated. There are some areas where disobedience is a problem. This time the evil forces had found and captured many vulnerabilities. When the pastor speaks to the congregation, they have to obey. Pastor Kim, do not worry, but visit her and deliver my message. My message is my will for her. Moreover, tell her to humble herself even more." The Lord reproached my wife. "When the time comes, your spiritual eyes are going to be surely opened. Why are you so impatient? Your spiritual eyes have not opened because there are still spiritual issues that you are not aware of. Later, you will naturally know the answer to what I am referring to."

Sister Baek, Bong-Nyu is really an unstoppable person. Generally, other believers who encounter Satan become frozen and diffident.

They become frightened and will not dare defy their enemy. However, Sister Baek Bong is very bold and she does not even blink her eyes at any place in hell. She is very strong and courageous. She has gradually influenced the other congregational members to become bold for the army of Jesus. All the members have become brave soldiers.

I went to the hospital to visit Sister Baek, Bong-Nyu. When I got there, she immediately said, "Pastor, I am so sorry that I had disobeyed you." She then told me that her operation had gone well. When she had fallen, her spinal cord had broken. Two of her vertebrae had broken and tore through the flesh. She had just received an operation that fastened her back with steel rods. She had six steel rods inserted into her back, three steel rods for each vertebrae.

I was very curious to why this was allowed to occur for one disobedience. She lived in poverty and I felt sorry for her. How would she cover the hospitalization bills and surgery? She was very pitiable.

The Lord watched silently in the midst of us. After a long time, He began to explain. Meticulously, He began to explain that every event that occurs to someone has a certain reason and underlying cause.

* Way Of The Lord, How Jesus Moves

Mrs. Kang, Hyun-Ja: My heart was in torment for a long time after Sister Baek, Bong-Nyu had become severely injured by the attack of the evil forces. An unbearable sadness had come upon me. I felt responsible for the accident. I was impatient and it was I who pushed us in haste. I desired our spiritual eyes to be opened so much. I continuously repented over and over. Jesus had already known that my heart was in torment. He comforted me by caressing my head and back.

In the afternoon, I quietly prayed in our small room and through the window an exceedingly fast beam of light shone down. In the midst of the light, Jesus had arrived. Whenever Jesus makes His entrance, a beam of light shines down. It is like a laser beam. It seems like He is traveling instantaneously at unimaginable speeds. There are no other entities that can travel like Jesus. Jesus is faster than any type of light, such as the rays of the sun or the illumination of a flashlight. He is not only faster, but He travels with precision.

Throughout my life, Jesus has always been with me. When He touches me, I could clearly feel His touch through my senses. Today, He showed me a very special scene. I finally realized how the Lord travels around the world so fast. He travels as fast as a flash. Before, I had vaguely thought about the idea. But now, I truly understand with certainty and I believe it with my heart. I understand how He knows the events of the world. Jesus oversees and watches the saints throughout the world. He does not have to travel around the world to know what is occurring with the saints. He already knows about them. It doesn't even take a second for Jesus to know the information of His saints.

The Lord said, "I show you this because I love you." I would expect that Jesus would show other believing saints the special secrets or various events because He loves everybody. "He that has my commandments, and keepeth them, he it is that loves me: and he that loveth me shall be loved of my Father, and I will love him, and will manifest myself to him." (John 14:21)

Whenever Jesus appears next to me, my surroundings become luminous and bright. It appears as though a bright pillar of light is in front of me. I always feel that Jesus is with me and is always accompanying me. The Pastor was delighting the Lord. "Oh Jesus! I love you!" The Lord said, "Pastor Kim! Since you have prayed all night, go and get some sleep." The Pastor replied with a unique and humorous expression on his face. "I love you." All of our family members laughed out loud.

From the Bible, we understand the characteristics of our Jesus as holy, serious, and graceful. It may appear that He is always discreet and would not be able to joke or be playful. Many people think the Lord is far from being humorous, jolly, or playful. However, when our spiritual eyes opened, we found out that He is great beyond our imagination. The closer we got to Him and as our spiritual eyes opened further, we found out He is humorous. But whenever we sinned, He grieved and lamented.

* Pastor Kim, You Are My True Bride

Today, when my husband went to sleep, the Lord appeared with some kind of sack cloth. Joseph, Joo Eun, and I were very surprised to see the Lord with a sack cloth. 'What is that? What is Jesus going to do?' We all watched carefully. It is usually the Pastor who entertains the Lord. Now, the Lord desired to have a wedding ceremony in heaven. The Lord said, "I suddenly desired to take the Pastor and have a wedding ceremony." The Lord then placed the Pastor's spirit into the sack cloth and returned to heaven with the Pastor's spirit. I did not know if the Pastor was aware of what had just happened. He was in a deep sleep. We started to chuckle to ourselves.

The Lord had a very unique and humorous facial expression as He took the Pastor's spirit within the sack cloth. We could not restrain from laughing. In heaven, the saints from the church of heaven came in groups to observe and laugh at the sight of the Lord bringing the Pastor in such a unique way. It almost appeared as though the Lord was kidnapping him. Jesus commanded the angels to dress and adorn the Pastor. The angels then took the pastor to the other room. They dressed and adorned him with precious stones and accessories. He looked great. The splendid wedding ceremony finally began. Once the ceremony ended, the reception began. The wedding reception started as the Pastor and Jesus danced in a humorous way. They were using their hips and moving side to side. All the saints were entertained. In fact, they were delighted that Father God laughed out loud in His deep voice.

The Pastor and Jesus danced for a long time. The Lord proclaimed, "From today, Pastor Kim, Yong-Doo is my true bride!" When the Lord proclaimed, all the saints shouted and clapped. The angels blew their trumpets and added merriment to the celebration. When the Lord danced hip to hip with the Pastor, it looked as though they were competing on who was dancing better. The Pastor's moves became progressively weird and strange. The Lord humorously said that it was hard to catch up to the Pastor's dance moves and that He would have to practice more. The Lord then returned back to our home. I asked the Lord: "Lord! Did you enjoy the wedding ceremony with Pastor Kim?" The Lord replied, "Of course, I liked it! I have wholly exposed the most inner parts of my heart to the Lord's Church! However, I wish the other churches would worship Me freely, with more interest and graciously." Jesus said that He would love to see all the churches worship and service in the Spirit more freely. Instead of being rigid and formal, He would like to see them be more flexible, entertaining, and blessed.

* Shower Down The Fireballs Of The Holy Spirit

Kim Joseph: As I prayed, large and small fireballs began to move around the throne of Father God. The fireballs began to shower down upon me. Initially, small fireballs showered down, but as time passed, the size of the fireballs gradually became larger. Eventually, the size of the fireballs became the size of houses and penetrated unceasingly into my body. As the fireballs entered my body, it was so hot that I could not bear the heat. "Oh, hot! Oh! Hot!" I shouted continuously.

I could see the gates of heaven widely open, especially today.

Jesus said that today was a special day for the saints of heaven to witness the events at the Lord's Church. The heavenly saints witnessed the worship, service, and the prayer rally. They were observing with great curiosity.

* The Saints In Heaven Come Down To Visit

Jesus had kept His word. During the middle of service, an extraordinarily shocking event took place. I was able to see several heavenly saints come down from heaven. With the Lord's command, they were able to visit us. I shouted loudly to the pastor: "Pastor! Pastor! Elijah the prophet has come down from heaven riding in a red chariot with fire horses. Wow! It's amazing! Look at the scene! They are hovering around the church ceiling. Following Elijah is Daniel and his three friends. I see Noah and Abraham coming as well!" The Pastor cringed and became startled.

The Pastor said, "Joseph! This event is very shocking and extraordinary. It can also create a lot of controversy. This even is huge and not in the Bible. There is a similar case, but not like this event. It did not involve many heavenly souls." The pastor then asked me to look up similar events in the Bible.

Pastor found Luke chapter 9:28-31. It was about Jesus praying at the mountain and His appearance had changed. Then Elijah and Moses had appeared. They had a conversation in regard to His departure. The Pastor was a bit doubtful. However, my little sister Joo-Eun surely witnessed the scene. Sister Baek, Bong-Nyu and Brother Haak Sung were busy witnessing the heavenly saints.

Jesus then shouted in an audible voice, "Is there anything that I cannot do? It is only the beginning. From now and forward, I will permit the heavenly saints to come and visit as much as I desire. Pastor Kim, you have to believe Me!" During our worship service, all of us dance, sing, and worship standing from our chairs as much as we desire. The Lord would also imitate our dances.

* Father God's Appearance As He Receives Our Worship

Father God, Jesus, and the Holy Spirit were impressed with our worship and service. When our church worships in service, we appear to be celebrating and entertaining. God was very delighted with our worship service. God always accepts our worship service pleasantly. As God watches over our worship service, He is very satisfied.

"And David danced before the LORD with all his might; and David was girded with a linen ephod. So David and all the house of Israel brought up the ark of the LORD with shouting, and with the sound of the trumpet. And as the ark of the LORD came into the city of David, Michal Saul's daughter looked through a window, and saw king David leaping and dancing before the LORD; and she despised him in her heart." (2 Samuel 6:14-16)

The Lord had Joo-Eun express movements in a dance. Jesus told Joo-Eun to move exactly as He moved and instructed her. We followed the dance movements of Jesus and moved in rhythm to the worship music that was being played from the mechanical piano. The Lord led us in dance and we freely worshipped much. A multitude of angles arrived from heaven to sit on the church chairs and they filled the church. Angels were also flying, occupying the air space as they watched. Generally, in any other day, evil spirits would hide in dark corners of the church, but today there were none.

Suddenly I became curious about Father God watching us. I wanted to know how He was reacting. As I was dancing, I looked up to heaven. Father God bounced to His feet and briefly moved from side to side. When Father God moved, an enormous flash or beam of light shined down. I could sense and feel that Father God was very pleased.

Father God moved in a unique and special way. With His enormous hand, He waved it from left to right. He then raised His other hand and moved it slowly from right to left. Father God continued to wave His big, mighty hands in the air. He then sat on His throne. He then stomped His right foot to the beat of the song that was playing in our church.

He laughed with a deep, sonorous voice. He then granted us a very special gift from the throne. A large ball that was bigger than a house began to roll toward me. The ball suddenly became a fireball and it entered my body. It was so hot that I almost instantly fainted. Blazing fireballs entered into all the members of our church. As the fireballs entered their bodies, the church members cried out and screamed, "Hot!"

* Seeing The Spiritual Realm With Our Physical Eyes

After church service, I returned home and witnessed evil spirits in our home. When I had opened the front entrance door to enter, groups of evil spirits that looked like mice ran from the master bedroom to the other small room. As my family members entered, the evil spirits rushed to move and hide in the corners. When I witnessed this event, I was seeing it with my physical eyes and it was very vivid. I also vividly saw Jesus with my eyes, which were opened at the church. The Lord had accompanied us as we returned home. He was with us. The Lord was radiating a golden color. He has brown hair. He was dressed in a radiant linen that glowed and His facial structure was fantastic.

We feel so comfortable and peaceful as we look upon our Lord who appears very benevolent and kind. His appearance gives us a sense of security.

Whether my eyes were opened or closed, I was able to see Jesus and Father God's throne. With my eyes closed, the sight was a bit blurred, but now with my eyes opened, it was very clear and vivid. Jesus said, "Joseph, I choose you as the man who will do great works for me at a later time. Therefore, I have granted you the ability to see the spiritual realm with your physical eyes as though they were your spiritual eyes."

I sometimes converse with the Lord as I clearly see him with my physical eyes. Sometimes Jesus looks like a physical man, but He can also come as a light to speak with me. Jesus said, "I will go to the house of prayer in the city of Hwa Sung to observe my servants praying. My servants gather there to pray together." He then instantly disappeared and later returned to me.

* Evangelizing To One Lost Soul

In the afternoon I briefly prayed at church and left to evangelize. I met a man and began to evangelize to him. He appeared very impressed as I evangelized to him. He listened to my message very carefully as he held the tract in his hand. He looked much older than me. He then spoke, "You know what? I've been mentally wandering around as different incidents have compounded in my life. They have all been bad. Thank you very much for sharing your message." He was determined to attend our church. Determined, he kept his word and is currently doing fine in his faith.

Jesus said that the reward for evangelizing is the most high. As He spoke, He added 150 stories to my home in heaven. I had been curious to know if my house was getting taller as I was granted rewards. I was able to confirm that my home was getting taller in heaven.

February 25th, 2005 (Friday)

Sermon scripture: "The Lord thy God in the midst of thee is mighty; he will save, he will rejoice over thee with joy; he will rest in his love, he will joy over thee with singing." (Zephaniah 3:17)

* The Service Is Ruined And The Lord Leaves

Mrs. Kang, Hyun Ja: Even before the service began, my daughter, Joo-Eun, was in an extremely bad mood and disturbing the peace. She has a hot temper. A hot tempered evil spirit was in her body. Finally the service was ruined by Joo-Eun. Even after ruining the service, Joo-Eun did not stop but vexed to the end. The service had become chilly within a short time and the service gradually became discordant. Worshipping had become awkward. The Pastor, who also has a quick temper, finally blew up. He had lost patience with her. Before the Pastor had blown up, I gave him the signal to be patient to the end. But the Pastor's quick and hot temper gave the evil spirits an advantage. The sermon was left unfinished and he had only spoken for 5 minutes.

There seems be no end to Joo-Eun's hysterical temper. She was stubborn and insisting on her way. The Pastor finally, harshly scolded her.

I do not know why my family members and I are so extremely stubborn. I am having a difficult time with our family's quick and hot temper.

The members of the church froze and their faces hardened. As this happened, my son, Joseph, and some other church members saw God's throne. Father God had bounced to his feet and was walking restlessly from side to side. Jesus said, "The service you are giving right now will not be received. No matter how many times, whether it be 100 or 1000 times — I will not receive it." After speaking, the Lord instantly disappeared.

The church members who had their spiritual eyes opened could not find Jesus or the Holy Spirit. They looked all around, but could not see our Lord. However, the forces of evil spirits swarmed and over-flowed into the place. They shouted and cheered and rejoiced as they clapped. "Wow! Good! Doing great! Wow I feel good! This is so great that I do not know what to do!" They were joyfully dancing and partying. The Pastor, with all the church members and myself, felt like our spiritual eyes had closed. We were not able to see. In that instance, an unbearable sadness came upon me. The Lord would not receive or delight in the service and preaching. The service and preaching was tainted with hot temper from members of the church. This was most revolting to the Lord.

* The Wrath Of Father God

As Brother Haak-Sung saw the throne, Father God had bounced up from His throne and appeared to be in full wrath. Furthermore, an enormously deep and frightening voice echoed. The voice of God vividly and sonorously echoed around Haak-Sung's ears. Father God's voice was like lightning and thunder. Father God proclaimed, "After I had opened your spiritual eyes, you have now become arrogant and conceited that you now lead your service so carelessly! If you ever lead a service in such a way, I will withdraw all the gifts from you!" Brother Haak- Sung said that he had never before felt so frighten by God. This was the first time he had actually felt frightened.

I could vividly feel God's wrath. Since we have come to a deep spiritual realm, we must be real careful about what God would think.

More eternal grace has been granted to us, and we need to humble ourselves even more. We need to live our lives holy. A small bit of complacency and carelessness can give the evil spirits strength to manifest their exploitations. The evil spirits would exploit a situation in which they can continue to escalate a problem or issue.

I thought to myself with doubt, 'surely not….one ruined service would not result in losing all our Holy gifts, would it?' I felt God was trying to teach us the importance of worship and service.

All churches have a bit of different worship and service. However, they are pretty much all the same. The services are apathetic and mixed with God's Word and tradition. Moreover, their tradition has been brought down from generation to generation. However, with proper training, teaching, and Bible study, Christians should know the importance of worship and service. They should realize and recognize the essence of service.

* Repenting By Slapping The Cheeks

As the congregation of the Lord's Church all repented with one loud voice, I heard someone continuously slapping himself. I, therefore, opened my eyes to investigate. It was the Pastor who was repenting with tears and slapping himself on the cheeks. "Lord! I have wrongly raised my child! I have not properly disciplined or educated her. As a result, I have sinned before you."

"He who spares his rod hates his son, but he who loves him disciplines him promptly." (Proverb 13:24)

The Pastor said, "Please forgive me, Lord." as he continuously slapped himself on the cheeks. The Pastor mercilessly slapped his cheeks. I thought to myself, 'What? How can he slap his own cheeks that hard?' As I thought to myself, my daughter, Joo-Eun ran toward the altar and kneeled next to the Pastor. She was the culprit who created the chaos. Joo-Eun then began repenting and crying. She also began slapping her own cheeks.

Joo-Eun has a difficult and uneasy personality. In some matters, she is so stubborn that once she is determined to do something, she will do it at all cost. She is extremely stubborn. Now I am not able to understand how a father and daughter can repent in the same extraordinary way. As Joo-Eun repented and slapped herself, she cried out: "God! Jesus! I have done wrong. Please forgive me! It is my fault that father is slapping himself in the cheeks. Please have him stop!" The Pastor continued to mercilessly slap his own cheeks as he cried out: "Lord! Please forgive me! It is also my fault. I also have a hot temper." I became worried as I saw Pastor continue to mercilessly slap himself. The congregation observed the Pastor and Joo-Eun repent and slap themselves. As a result, the congregation prayed more aggressively.

Jesus had left for some time but He had returned again. He silently stood from a distance and observed us repent. He was observing the Pastor and Joo-Eun with careful attention. Several days later, the Lord kindly spoke to us. The Lord said that Father God was very angry. The Lord then warned us with a message that if we ever give another worship service in such a careless or ill manner, the Father will deal with us harshly.

As Joo Eun listened to Jesus's direct words, she confessed. "Jesus! Jesus! I am very sorry. I have done wrong! Please forgive me." The Lord spoke to her and hugged her tightly. "Alright, do not behave in such a way ever again." Jesus also hugged the Pastor and advised the Pastor not to scold his children in every single matter but to educate them with love. Jesus said that in order to relieve Father God's anger and heart completely, we would have to pray in repentance a little more.

After some time had passed, with morning approaching, the Lord told us to break and eat some snack. He commanded us to joyously worship again.

Kim, Joseph: While I was in prayer, Jesus returned. Unlike other days, the Lord's facial expression was that of anger. In fact, it was a bit frightening. I was apprehensive and scared. I had never seen the Lord with that facial expression before. I think it was probably because of Joo-Eun and Pastor's temper that had ruined the service.

Jesus said, "Joseph, let us go to hell!" As soon as Jesus held my hand, I was instantly in hell. The Lord would sometimes either take me there instantly to the center of hell or He would take me through the trip to meticulously experience the journey. When we reached the center of hell, I gazed steadily to locate the chair where Satan sat. I concentrated to observe the events and surroundings. As I observed, I could no longer watch with my eyes. The scene was horrific and cruel.

* A Room Full Of Death Weapons

The king of devils, Satan, sat on his throne and directed his subordinates. Satan's subordinates were busy moving about, accomplishing his commands. Some were walking and some were flying in the air. Their numbers were countless and the operation was sophisticated; I was unable to comprehend what was going on. The evil spirits were organized into a system of hierarchy. One gave an order and one would receive and execute. All the levels incorporated ranks.

There was a table in front of Satan. The table was covered with various weapons of death. In fact, there were so many, it looked like mountains. The weapons included old time, worn farm equipment, conventional weapons, and armaments. Other various weapons were also included. Satan's subordinates would take a weapon from the table to stab, lacerate, and spear at their victims. However, the evil spirits were not satisfied. They would go to another place in hell to bring more and different types of death weapons.

I was in an enormous room with many dividing walls. There were various, brutal weapons hanging on the wall. Such weapons were weapons one can only see in movies, books, Sci Fi, and fiction stories. They were weapons of imagination from the earth. As I observed the variety of weapons hanging on the wall, I felt as though I was looking at some tool exhibition. As the evil spirits grabbed a death weapon to chop off the legs of people, it reminded me when my friends and I had casually torment insects and ants. The evil spirits found it joyous and entertaining as they chopped the legs off people to watch them in torment.

As Jesus pointed to the people who were lined up to be tormented, He said, "Among these souls are some who participated in a cult. There are some who were alcoholics and some who treated the Sabbath or Sunday carelessly. On Sundays they would spend money for their pleasure. Most of these people are here for not keeping Sundays Holy. There are some who ran businesses and assumed that the Lord would forgive them. They were deceived."

The Lord continued to explain that among the group were elders and deaconesses. In fact, there are countless number of deacons, deaconesses, and pastors. He showed this to me very clearly. There were also many different ethnic groups, all different races. There were blacks, whites, and people from my country. I was very surprised to see many people who looked similar to me. A large majority were Asians. I was astonished to notice how I was able to distinguish the different ethnic groups.

Suddenly, I became frightened and startled. I screamed loudly, "Jesus! Jesus! I really hate hell. Please do not let the evil spirits come toward me! Jesus then grabbed my hand. I returned back to church and continued to pray.

Since we did not please the Lord with our first worship service, we began a second worship service. Before the second worship service, we repented and then started worship. With repentance, our second worship service was fervent and harmonious. We had restored our worship and service. Trinity God was very pleased.

* The Newspaper And A Picture In Heaven

Thinking about Jesus, I danced and worshipped. I danced freely. All the members who had their spiritual eyes opened soon shouted. Something had come down from heaven.
"Wow! What is this? Is it a newspaper? What! Heaven has a newspaper? Wow! Newspapers are coming down from heaven." I was the first one to shout. A gold color light shone from the edges of the newspaper. The edges were also decorated with precious stones. The words were printed with pearls. The center of the newspaper had vivid pictures of the congregation of the Lord's Church worshipping, giving service, and dancing in the spirit.

As I watched the scene, I was amazed at what was happening. It was surreal. The members who did not have their spiritual eyes opened were perplexed. They had a difficult time comprehending what we were describing. The event was outstanding and too good to miss out on. It was a bit sad because the ones without opened spiritual eyes were missing out on something great.

As I looked at the pictures, I noticed that each member had a unique appearance and expression of their own. The headline of the Heavenly newspaper stated, "The Lord"s Church praying." The size of the letters for the headline was huge. One of the pictures had the Pastor's face in the center. The pictures were very similar to the ones we would take here on earth. We were smiling by stating, "cheese."

* Jesus Promoting The Lord's Church

Jesus said, "Joseph! What do you think? You have never seen this, right?" Jesus had personally commanded the angels to print the newspapers and He had commanded the saints in heaven to distribute them to read. Jesus said that if He commands the heavenly saints to read, they have no choice but to read. He also had said that it was very rare that a church from earth would be in heaven's newspaper. However, the Lord's Church frequently appears in heaven's newspaper.

Jesus asked me once again, "Observe closely. Do you think the pictures had come out well?" As I looked closely again, I laughed for a long time. I noticed the facial expressions of the church members who had their spiritual eyes opened; they were very unique. The pictures were amazing. The members who had opened spiritual eyes were busy explaining with great excitement to the members with unopened spiritual eyes.

The Lord explained how He went around in Heaven to announce and advertise my father, the Pastor. Jesus explained how He would announce the pastor. "There is a new, small church in the city of Suh, Incheon. The name of the church is the Lord's Church. The church is led by one pastor. Whenever he preaches or worships, he makes a lot of humorous facial expressions or gestures." I, myself, agree. My father does make a lot of comical facial expressions or gestures.

* Fire Of The Holy Spirit

Pastor Kim, Yong-Doo: While I was in prayer time, I focused on the Lord to go deeper. I shouted and cried out to the Lord. Previously, a short time ago, I had repented by slapping my cheeks. As a result, my cheeks are swollen and hot. They felt like they were on fire.

Without the Holy fire, my cheeks were already hot. But when the Holy Fire entered my body, my cheeks began to cook. It felt as though my body was placed on top of a hot stove, a stove with tremendous heating power. The healing hand gestures gradually became stronger and faster. My hands produced various motions. After two hours had passed, enormous, hot fireballs suddenly entered into my body through the tip of my fingers. I could not bear it. The fire gradually spread throughout my body.

My body was so hot that I had to scream. My legs kicked and fluttered due to the intense heat. I had reached my limit; I was burning with thirst. "Water! Water! Does anybody have water?" I then drank like someone who had not drank for days.

* Poisonous Thorns Of The Holy Spirit

Kim, Joseph: Once my spiritual eyes were opened, and as I continued to go spiritually deeper, the evil spirits would place outrageous obstacles before me. The obstacles are unfamiliar and so numerous that I could no longer count. Compared to the other church members, it took a long time for me to go spiritually deeper. The Lord explained that I was called to be a pastor. I had realized that an enormous price is paid to have one's spiritual eyes opened. Whenever I longed and desired to go deeper spiritually, I was mercilessly attacked. The evil spirits would look for any weakness or gaps to attack. And through my weakness and gaps, I was occasionally defeated through their attacks.

Evil spirits would frequently enter my body. The other members of our church would also be continuous targets by the evil spirits. Once the evil forces enter our bodies, the unbearable pain and torment would begin.

I asked the Lord, "Jesus! Whenever the evil spirits enter our bodies, we are in torment and pain. Do other members from other churches experience the same pain as we do?" The Lord replied, "Some may experience pain and torment, but not at the level that the members of the Lord's Church experience. Generally, most people do not feel pain and torment. The evil spirits secretly hide within their body and clandestinely plot."

I asked once again: "Lord! Grant us the poisonous holy thorns so that the evil spirits cannot enter our bodies. We can use it to prevent them from entering us?" Jesus then commanded us to shout in unison: "Poisonous thorns of the Holy Spirit! Please grant us poisonous thorns of the Holy Spirit!"

When I had asked the Lord for the poisonous thorns of the Holy Spirit, I was only being playful and not serious. But I found out that there is really such a gift or power. I could never have had imagined it in my dreams. "Pastor! Pastor! Is there such a word as the 'poisonous thorns of the Holy Spirit' mentioned in the Bible?" The Pastor replied, "Joseph! There are no such words mentioned like that in the Bible." However, the Lord had not only showed us, but He did state, that although it was not mentioned in the Bible, the poisonous thorn of the Holy Spirit did exist.

Jesus granted us the poisonous thorns of the Holy Spirit. The poisonous thorns stuck out from our bodies with sharp points. Pastor said, "Joseph! Why is my body tingling?" As I checked the Pastor's body, his body was covered with many thorns. He reminded me of a hedgehog. I explained to the Pastor that his thorns were much bigger and stronger. In fact, his thorns were more poisonous than the congregation members's. The Lord had always granted the Pastor stronger gifts and power.

The other members of our church also possessed the poisonous thorns of the Holy Spirit in our body. Whenever we shout "Poisonous thorns of the Holy Spirit" numerous thorns from inside our bodies would appear.

* Pricked By The Poisonous Thorns

Pastor Kim, Yong Doo: Without opened spiritual eyes, I was not able to view the poisonous thorns of the Holy Spirits. However, I wanted to investigate and see what the poisonous thorns on my body were all about. There is no word "Poisonous thorn of the Holy Spirit" in any of the 66 books in the Bible. I wanted to verify the words of Joseph and the other congregational members. My physical senses were telling me that I did experience a tingling sensation. But I am a character of needing to see, feel, and experience to be certain. My mind was filled with determination to verify this event.

As the evil spirits attacked, we would daily experience the power of the poisonous thorns on our body. The evil spirits were turned to ashes. As the evil spirits got pricked, they would turn to ashes. At one time, I had asked the youngsters to close their eyes. With their eyes closed, I lightly touched my daughter, Joo-Eun's hand with the tip of my finger. The moment I touched her, Joo-Eun screamed loudly and fell on the floor. "Ouch! Pastor! Father! Why are you pricking me with the poisonous thorns?" She shouted and cried. After pricking Joo-Eun, followed by Yoo-Kyung, Haak-Sung and Joseph, got pricked by me. However, I barely grazed their bodies, but every one of them fell to the floor. The area where I had grazed them with my finger began to swell and the poison began to gradually spread throughout their bodies. They became paralyzed. I had personally witnessed this event.

"Pastor, Pastor! Hurry! Hurry! Pray for us, now! Please stop the poison from spreading throughout our bodies!" I replied, "What? How am I suppose to stop it?" They shouted, "Stop it! Touch us with your hands!" I shouted back, "No! If I touch you again, the poison will enter you again and maybe spread faster. Don't you agree?" The youngsters cried and fell onto the floor one at a time. They said, "No! It is all right. Lay your hands on us with the heart of praying!" As I prayed, I had just barely prevented the poison from spreading throughout their bodies and they were relieved of their pain.

As I thought to myself, I did not know how to accept this event. I was not able to explain what had just happened. I was perplexed and the situation felt absurd. After this incident, the youngsters avoided me and dared not come close to me.

As we prayed, our bodies became covered with poisonous thorns. The evil spirits, not knowing, attacked and became ash as they got pricked by the thorns. They had become ash and disappeared. However, the strong evil spirits did not turn to ash so easily. They were able to make numerous attempts to enter our bodies — even after being pricked by the thorns. The Lord had sometimes taken the thorns away to make sure we did not become complacent with our prayers. We could not just depend on the poisonous thorns of the Holy Spirit but had to combine it with prayer: "People of the Lord's Church! The poisonous thorns are not all that powerful. You cannot rely on them completely. The poisonous thorns were a temporary expedient to battle the evil spirits. I grant them to you since you are repeatedly attacked. Defeat the evil spirits with your strong faith rather than depending on the poisonous thorns."

* Saint Kang, Hyun-Ja Is A Special Fiancée Unto The Lord

Mrs. Kang, Hyun-Ja: Several years ago, by the Lord's grace, I was led to heaven. At that time, as I looked at myself, I was not much to look at. However, countless beautiful bridesmaids appeared and approached toward me. They beautifully dressed me.

The status of Jesus is a fiancé who will become the bridegroom. My status is the fiancée. We have a relationship that no one can possibly keep us apart. We are so in love. My physical love for my physical husband is nothing compared to the love I have with the Lord.

With the daily cares of life, I had forgotten the heavenly visitation. I later found out that the Lord had not forgotten about me. My beloved Lord had always been accompanying me. Moreover, He had sometimes watched me sleep. Whenever I slept too long, He would say, "My fiancée, why are you sleeping so long? Why do you leave me alone?" When He expresses His jealous love, I instantaneously soak in happiness. It is a happiness I cannot express or describe with words.

My beloved Lord always accompanies all the believers. With my spiritual eyes, I have clearly seen that He does accompany all believers. When I told my husband what I had experienced, He said that the Lord loves all believers equally.

As the Lord silently listened to our conversation, He touched my head and sent me a signal. The Holy Spirit numerously accompanies the pastor. He touches the pastor"s head and face many times. The Lord accompanies me many times as well. I am gradually going deeper as my spiritual eyes are now partially opened.

Whenever the pastor is comical and is a bit harsh with his jokes, the Lord always intervenes. "Pastor Kim, do not treat my fiancée so roughly." As the Lord commented, my husband hesitantly said, "I am living with a wife whose heart is far from me." The pastor laughed out loud. The Lord and I then laughed together. As we all laughed together, I realized that one day is not enough time to spend with the Lord.

Chapter 3
Holy Electricity

February 28th, 2005 (Monday)

Sermon scripture: "A new heart also will I give you, and a new spirit will I put within you: and I will take away the stony heart out of your flesh, and I will give you a heart of flesh. And I will put my spirit within you, and cause you to walk in my statutes, and ye shall keep my judgments, and do them." (Ezekiel 36:26-27)

* Pink Colored Heart Shaped Bubbles Expressing The Heart Of Love

Kim, Joseph: As I was earnestly yearning for Jesus, some extraordinary beings came out of my body. I was very surprised. I tightly closed my eyes and prayed but the phenomenon did not go away. Pink colored bubbles came out of my body. They were shinning and beaming. As they continuously came out of my body, the pink bubbles transformed into heart-shaped forms. They flew up toward heaven to the throne of God. As they passed space, they traveled through the galaxy and finally reached God's throne. They appeared fragile, like standard air bubbles, and appeared as though they would easily pop with any slight impact. As I watched, I felt nervous that they would pop. But fortunately, they did not pop.

With a resounding, deep echoing voice, Father God impressively said, "Hmmm, Joseph's heart is coming up! Very well, thank you!" He then received the heart-shaped bubbles. God was very pleased and satisfied as He laughed. The pink hearts represent my heart toward God. Once they reach Father God, they would gush forth a fantastic light before God. Within a short time, similar shaped bubbles began to come forth from God toward me.

"Since you have given me your loving heart, I will also give you my heart!" From the bosom of God, beautiful shaped hearts lighted with pink endlessly came down. They were incomparable to my heart-shaped bubbles. When God's heart-shaped bubbles endlessly entered my body, my heart raced in excitement and overflowed with happiness.

I said to Father God: "Father God! Thank you for loving me so much. I used to be greedy and fretful. I was impatient and wanted my spiritual eyes opened hastily." Before I could finish my sentence, Father God said, "It is all right! Today, this phenomenon proves that you and I have the same loving heart and the manifestation of faith." After this experience, I always think about God and I am always in prayer.

* The Lord Who Gives Sleep To Saints

Mrs. Kang, Hyun-Ja: "Lord! These days, I am having a difficult time falling asleep after an all night prayer. I want to sleep, but I am in torment and cannot fall asleep. Lord, I need to sleep well in order to get rid of the fatigue. Please help me sleep well!" My daughter who was next to me shouted: "Mother! Jesus is giving you a hug." As soon as He held me in His arms, I gently fell asleep. I fell asleep as though I was either intoxicated with sleeping pills or anesthetics. As I fell deeper in sleep, the Holy Spirit was a hot, soft energy that soaked and heated into my body.

"It is vain for you to rise up early, to sit up late, to eat the bread of sorrows: for so he giveth his beloved sleep." (Psalms 127:2)

Jesus continues to tell the members of the Lord's Church that His heart has opened up widely to the Lord's Church. The Lord had especially made my kids and I very happy. He is sometimes playful and would come mirthfully. The Lord sometimes wears an extraordinary looking outfit or comes in a comical appearance. The purpose of his theatrical visit was to make us happy. I am sometimes confused as to whether who is to make who happy. The Lord loved our worship and service very much. He said that He always waits for our church to worship and service.

Since the Lord's Church and my family relentlessly focus on Trinity God, our laughter never ends. Our hearts speak to the Lord. Our important topics for discussion are always the Lord. All of our conversation is God centered. We notice the Lord almost and always is accompanied by the Holy Spirit, but sometimes He operates alone.

March 4th, 2005 (Friday)

Sermon scripture: "And he called unto him the twelve, and began to send them forth by two and two; and gave them power over unclean spirits; And commanded them that they should take nothing for their journey, save a staff only; no scrip, no bread, no money in their purse: But be shod with sandals; and not put on two coats. And he said unto them, In what place soever ye enter into a house, there abide till ye depart from that place. And whosoever shall not receive you, nor hear you, when ye depart thence, shake off the dust under your feet for a testimony against them. Verily I say unto you, It shall be more tolerable for Sodom and Gomorrha in the day of judgment, than for that city. And they went out, and preached that men should repent. And they cast out many devils, and anointed with oil many that were sick, and healed them." (Mark 6:7-13)

* The Tongue Of The Devil

Mrs. Kang, Hyun-Ja: During the early morning prayer meeting, as I earnestly prayed in tongues, a strange sound began coming out of my mouth. Two hours had passed. Initially, I was excited with the new and different sound in tongues. I thought the Lord had granted me another tongue. The sound of the new tongue gradually became strange. My intuition was telling me that something was wrong.

My body became covered up with goose bumps. Finally, an evil laugh by a young woman came out. "Oh, hohohoho, hohoholoholoholo, eeheeeheeeeheee, ehehehehe." All different varieties of evil laughter continuously gushed out. At the same time, Sister Baek, Bong-Nyu also began speaking with the devil's tongues. She sounded exactly like the girl who was demonized in the popular movie, "The Exorcist"

I thought to myself. 'How can the devil's tongues come out from my mouth?' No matter how much I thought about it, I could not understand it. The sound of the devil's tongues would not stop. Within a short time, my head began to gradually move side to side. Then the speed accelerated. My head began to shake violently and I could not stop it.

I opened my eyes and saw Sister Baek, Bong-Nyu also shaking violently. Finally, our Pastor, who was praying, somehow sensed what was happening and immediately came to us. He then began to cast the demons out. "Satan! Depart! Spirit of confusion — depart in the name of Jesus!"

Before this manifestation, I was not concentrating during my prayer in tongues. In fact, I was thinking about other things. During that moment of my weakness, the demons used that opportunity to come into my body. This is why my tongues turned into the demon's. Whenever the demons come into my body, I am always in torment. I am not only physically affected, but I get mentally confused and become very tired. As the Pastor walked back and forth between Sister Baek, Bong-Nyu and myself, he prayed over us. And whenever the Pastor prays over me, I become normal. However, when he walked away toward Baek, Bong-Nyu to pray over her, the devil's tongue began to come out of my mouth again.

* The Forces Of Evil Spirits Enter Into Mrs. Kang, Hyun-Ja's Body

"Jesus! Jesus! Why are the devil's tongues manifesting continuously?" But the Lord kept silent. The Lord is sweet and kind, but He was not speaking a word this time. He stood silently and watched us.

Once again, I broke my concentration and thought about something else. In that moment, the evil spirits came back into my body as a group. I almost passed out. My body began to go numb. I then began to tumble on the floor in pain. No matter how much I cried out and pleaded, the Lord did not respond. It was futile.

Sister Baek, Bong-Nyu was also tumbling on the floor and crying in pain. The Pastor became nervous and his face turned pale. He continued to walk back and forth between us while he prayed. His physical strength was at his limit. He was totally exhausted. The Pastor is usually very confident when it comes to his stamina. However, as he would cast out evil spirits, shouting and screaming, he had become very tired as he had to go back and forth to Sister Baek, Bong-Nyu and me. Moreover, the Pastor's wounds from the evil spirits in previous battles were not completely healed. As a result, he suffered more and was in additional agony. However, despite his wounds, he continued to pray unceasingly for us. I felt sorry for the Pastor, and I wanted him to rest, but not before helping me. I asked him to pray for me since my pain was unbearable. The attacks had been continuous. It has already been 4 or 5 days. I had been relentlessly attacked. I was harassed day and night. I was not able to eat, drink or sleep at all. I had been the victim of relentless attacks more than the others. I could not rest.

* The Lord's Preliminary Announcement About The Ministry Of Holy Fire And Deliverance

Jesus was about to explain why He stood silent as we pleaded and pitifully shouted for Him. We were shouting and asking for help in driving out the evil spirits.

I asked the Lord why He had allowed the evil spirits to enter my body continuously. I told Him that the pain I was experiencing was unbearable. The Lord began to explain. "There are several different reasons why I am allowing these things. The first reason is to mend your bad habits of compulsively speaking and divulging information. Saint Kang, Hyun-Ja! You are my beloved fiancé. When the proper time is allowed, everything will be revealed. Spiritual secrets must be kept secret, but you go around telling everyone in all places. Do you not think you need to change your ways? You definitely will not change by my words! This is why I am allowing these events to discipline you. Through this painful experience, you will be changed!"

When I reminisce upon myself, I am far from changed. I wonder how much more deplorable I appear in the Lord's eyes. Once I had realized this, I became so shameful that I wanted to hide.

Jesus continued: "In the future, there will be a time when people will experience the Holy Blazing Fire worldwide. The Lord's Church will lead the momentum of the work of the Holy Fire. I will make you lead and perform the Fire ministry. However, you will have to receive and experience many trials to be trained. But do not be afraid when you face many trials. Boldly endure it!"

The Lord added, "You must know and understand the evil spirit's schemes and strategies in order to evict and cast them out. You must know their plans in depth. You will have to experience the torment and oppression first hand so that you will understand the pain and torment of other people who are oppressed by the forces of darkness. You will genuinely feel sorry for them as you will know their pain. You will be motivated to heal and deliver them. This is why I have allowed your experience!"

"But unto you I say, and unto the rest in Thyatira, as many as have not this doctrine, and which have not know the depths of Satan, as they speak; I will put upon you none other burden. But that which ye have already hold fast till I come." (Revelation 2:24-25)

All things that occur on this earth must require some sacrifice. Generally, things or matters do not go smoothly without sacrifice. In the spirit realm, an enormous price must be paid to learn or earn something. The Lord's Church had especially encountered many evil spirits in which we battled endlessly.

If we are not prepared to battle against the evil forces, we will eventually be defeated. I have come to realize that the congregation of our church had been nominated as somewhat of an experiment. Every day we fight against the evil spirits in the spirit realm. And every day we are baptized by the Holy Fire as well. We were not only just an experiment, but this experience trained us in discernment and immunity.

However, on the other hand, the spiritual battles have been something unexpected and beyond our imagination. As the battles are continuous and endless, as our physical bodies become exhausted, I now envy the people who live normal Christian lives. They appear happy to me. As we receive many gifts, more each day, and as our spiritual eyes are continuously opened, we become the center of the devil's attack. We become his targets. With that said, we also become the center of criticisms from others. We are misunderstood and people become jealous of us. We are the center of all battles both spiritual and with other people. The battles are relentless: it is daily. However, now, we have become accustomed to such matters.

Generally, people would think that having their spiritual eyes opened would be great and joyous. It may appear somewhat good, but in reality, it is totally the opposite. When one is in the spiritual realm, one must become much stronger than when we are in the physical realm. In the spiritual realm, one can only be approved if one wins the battle on a daily basis. However, it is very difficult to live spiritually in all areas. It is most difficult and cumbersome when the physical body cannot keep pace with the occurrences in the spirit.

Despite the difficulties, however, it is still great to have special favor and attention. We are all approved by Him. We are able to taste the pleasant sensation of victory and joy. Moreover, it is an abundantly thrilling. The excitement cannot be experienced from the world. In fact, it is eternal happiness.

Before my spiritual eyes were opened, I was ignorant of all the events and experiences I had encountered. My faith was based on theory and academics. One thing is for sure, one cannot conclude that their spiritual eyes are opened just because one has received a holy gift. When you battle evil spirits, you have to defeat them, otherwise, you will be immediately defeated. If you do not harm your opponent, they will enormously harm you.

The spiritual war has resulted in many pastors and their wives to be deceived. As a result, their deception and failure have led them to hell. We are witnessing and experiencing the spiritual war. I am also the wife of a pastor. And as a pastor's wife, I wanted to support and serve my pastor much better than any other pastor's wife. Actually, that goal was very difficult to do. There were many times before where I had presented or judged situations through my experiences and my flesh. Before, the humanism soaked into my heart; therefore, I used to judge all matters from my point of view.

Whenever I was oppressed and hopelessly attacked by evil forces for several days, I would be defeated. I would not be able to eat and the condition of my misery would continue. Just like a crazy person, I would lose my mind and my body would shake violently. As I experienced these painful situations, I am now able to relate to the pain and misery of multitudes of people who are afflicted and oppressed by evil spirits through the world.

As I was in unbearable torment, I pleaded to the Lord. I saw the Lord's face; he was watching me with the expression of a stone. It brought me much sadness to witness his expression. Perhaps, Jesus is letting me experience various trails for some future event or events.

* 150 Evil Spirits Enter Once Again

How much more will the Lord continue to test us and until when? During the second prayer meeting, about 150 evil spirits entered my body once more. The tongue from the devil began to unceasingly come out from my mouth. The evil spirits began to numb my whole body, including all of my joints and bones. It started at 9 p.m. and the Pastor and I struggled until noon the next day which was 12 p.m.

I shouted and cried out to the Lord. As I realized that I did not have enough faith to cast them out of my body, I cried and cried. I was shameful. As the pastor's wife, my faith was only at a mediocre level. This is why I must be continuously harassed by the evil spirits. As I pondered these thoughts to myself, I cried out even more. Why were these evil spirits attacking me, especially me? Why I am not able to cast the evil forces out with my faith? I became emotional with contempt and was falling apart. My soul/spirit shook with uncertainty. Due to exhaustion, the other church members went home. The Pastor and I were the only ones remaining. The Pastor took a few steps backwards and said, "Ah! They are awful! I have done many deliverances, but I have never experienced such tenacious evil spirits like these before — very stubborn!"

As I cried, I pleaded to the Pastor. "Honey! What should I do? You must cast them out." The Pastor replied: "All right, I understand already! However, let me rest a bit and I can do it again." After the Pastor held his breath, he sat me on a bench as he sat behind me on the back rail with his legs over my shoulders. The Pastor then laid his hand on me and began to pray. As he prayed, he opened my mouth with his fingers and all different kinds of evil spirits began to gush forward one at a time.

The Pastor and I became gradually exhausted. We were one step from passing out. Moreover the Lord continued to just observe us. I think He wanted to observe and wait until our limit was reached. The filthy, ugly evil spirits absolutely had no sign of fatigue. In fact, they gradually screamed louder. Now, they were attacking us as though wild beasts attacked prey. We could no longer bear it, We had run all out of our spiritual and physical strength. When the Pastor shouted, "Holy Fire!" we heard the evil spirits constantly shout, "Ah, hot! Ah hot! Ah hot! However, when the Pastor's voice weakened, the evil spirits became more violent in my body. During the middle of battle, we recorded the sounds to leave evidence.

As the Lord watched, He might have felt sorry for us because He had finally intervened. Jesus entered the Pastor's body. As soon as the Lord entered his body, the Pastor gained strength once more and was fill in fullness with the Holy Spirit. The Pastor then cast all the evil spirits out. I was finally able to rest. The Lord said, "All these experiences are necessary so that you can be used globally at a later time. The Lord then explained it in more detail.

Without the Lord's help, we are weak vessels that are not able to perform anything at any given time. We can only perform properly when the Lord intervenes or works on our behalf. Our bodies were very tired and exhausted. But we thanked the Lord. We finally made it home around 3 p.m.

* Experimental Nominees

Pastor Kim, Yong-Doo: My wife and Sister Baek, Bong-Nyu were big targets for the evil forces to attack. Almost on a daily basis, I desperately struggled with the evil spirits as they entered their bodies. Usually, when the evil spirits infiltrate into peoples's bodies, it would only take a brief moment to easily and speedily enter them. However, once they had entered someone's body, it was never easy for them to go.

Some evil spirits are very strong and they have their own strategies to defend themselves. They rigorously resist and scream during the burning of the Holy Blazing Fire. Whenever the evil spirits are forced to leave our bodies, they may harm our bodies and leave serious side effects or after effects.

Because of the Lord's grace, I was able to clearly count the number of evil forces. Joseph, Joo-Eun, Haak-Sung, and Yoo-Kyung's spiritual power escalated to a higher level and now they were able to fight against evil spirits. The Lord had especially protected the youngsters, but the adults like my wife, Sister Baek, Bong-Nyu, and I were left to handle difficult situations. After battling evil spirits every day, I became so exhausted and felt like every inch of my strength had run out. Still, the Lord only observed without assisting. From the mouth of my wife, all different, various, appalling sounds were coming out: the various sounds of a young girl's wail and the sound of wild beasts. I could have never imagined that these different kinds of evil spirits could exist, especially, when I witnessed my wife hissing like a snake with her tongue. When I saw that, my body was covered with goose bumps and my hairs rose. "Shhhh…Shhhhh! Ohohohoh!" When I heard the sound of a young girl mournfully crying, I shivered in fear — it was so creepy and strange.

I had found out later that all of our church members were experiments. The Lord later explained it to us in detail. He explained it to us more vividly to help us understand.

* The Burnt Ashes Of Evil Spirits Revived

The evil spirits had the ability to revive themselves even after we had burned them with fire — the fire from the Holy Spirit. I had cast and burnt all the evil spirits from the bodies of my wife and Sister Baek, Bong-Nyu. However, instead of the evil spirits being burned and gone, they began to scream.

They shouted with the human characteristic voices. "No, No! I won't leave! Why would I leave when it is so nice here! Why would I leave? Ouch, Ouch! Hot! Hot! The Holy Fire is coming in once more! Ouch! Hot! I can"t bear it! Pastor Kim, you @#%#@%$! Take your hands off! All right, all right! I will get out. I am leaving. I am leaving!" They said they would leave many times. In fact, hundreds of times they said it. Later, they had become ash.

When they became ashes, I relaxed my guard and thought, "It must really be finished." However, the ashes began to reform to another kind of evil spirit. It revived! "What! How can this happen? What are these? I am sick and tired!" My kids also began to yell, "Pastor! We have a serious problem! The evil spirits have revived. Big problem! What should we do?" In an audible voice, I spoke some encouragement. "What do you mean, what we ought to do? We are starting all over again. Cast them all out!" I then began battling the evil spirits that were in Sister Baek, Bong-Nyu and my wife. I felt as though the battle was endless. "Hey guys! Do not be taken off guard. Gather yourselves and do not stand in the way where the evil spirits are leaving! Stay real close behind me and pray."

Whenever the evil spirits leave one's body, they go into the body of saints who are weak in faith. The other saints with weak faiths should not be in close proximity. Otherwise, they have to be on guard and ready. As I continued to attack the burned evil spirits that were nothing but a heap of ashes, they eventually turned into dark smoke. The smoke wriggled and finally disappeared to hell. My wife suffered for about four days from the after affects. She groaned in pain as well. Sister Baek, Bong-Nyu was also in the same condition. However, when evening services were about to begin, the Lord had always granted them the grace to recover. With the Lord's recovery grace, the two looked very peaceful and full of grace when they danced in the Holy Spirit.

* God Dances

Lee, Haak-Sung: After we had cast out all evil spirits from Mrs. Kang, Hyun-Ja and my mother, we fervently sang worship songs once again. We then began our individual prayers. A vision began to appear in front of my eyes. I saw a vision of God's throne. Joseph and I were looking at the throne of God at the same time.

Father God stood up from His throne and reenacted the dance we had danced at our worship service. Due to the beam of light, we could not still see Father's face. However, we were able to see Him dance. Father unfolded His enormous right index finger and shook it from side to side. He moved about and danced. He then unfolded His left index finger and shook it side from side. Father swayed His legs and whenever they swayed, all different shapes and colors of the rainbow poured down.

Moses came up to God's throne and said to himself. "Oh, Father God does not act in such fashion. Why is God dancing?" Father God instantly spoke and commanded Moses: "Moses! Moses! I am very delighted by the worship of the Lord"s church. I am very joyous! Why don't you dance as well?" As soon as God spoke, Moses danced before God for quite a long time. God said, "I feel so great today!" God was joyous and pleased. Moses danced awkwardly at first, but began to dance delightfully. I thought Father God only received our services, worship, and prayers. However, He expresses His delightfulness and dances. The sight was really unbelievable.

Even after witnessing such a wonderful experience, Father God continues to dance whenever we worship at the church. Father God would also stomp His foot up and down in excitement and mirth. The sound of stomping echoed all throughout the sky and the light of joy would spread in all directions. Whenever God was delighted, the twenty four elders in front of God, the saints in heaven, and the angels would also be delighted. The angels would blow the trumpets.

March 6th, 2005 (Sunday)

Sermon scripture: "The Spirit of the Lord God is upon me; because the Lord hath anointed me to preach good tidings unto the meek; he hath sent me to bind up the brokenhearted, to proclaim liberty to the captives, and the opening of the prison to them that are bound" (Isaiah 61:1)

* Heaven's Recorder And Camcorder

Kim, Joo-Eun: I fervently worshipped during worship service. In the middle of worship, a light suddenly shone down. I saw a procession of lights with multitude of angles coming down. "Wow! Pastor, sisters, brothers, many angels are coming down!" I shouted.

The angels brought some various objects with them. The smaller objects were in their hands while the bigger ones were on their shoulder. The objects were recorders and camcorders. The recorders and camcorders were decorated with precious stones and were made of gold. As a matter of fact, they were pretty nice looking. The moment I saw them, I wanted to have one of each camera.

The angels were recording every event that was occurring at our church. "Wow! How could this be happening? I would have never guessed that heaven would take pictures and record like we do here on earth." I was amazed and thought it was very novel. I continued to shout. I had never seen anything like this in my life. "Brother Joseph! Brother Haak-Sung, Sister Yoo- Kung! Look at that! Wow! Amazing!"

There were some angels that recorded the Pastor's humorous facial expressions and gestures during his sermon and worship. It appeared as though people from a broadcasting station were shooting the scenes. As Jesus followed the Pastor, He imitated the

Pastor's humorous and unique facial expressions. The angels were very busy walking around and shooting the facial expressions and gestures of the congregation.

The cameras, camcorders, and recorders looked very similar to the ones we have here except that they were made of gold and decorated with the precious stones of heaven. However, we did not know what the purpose was for recording and shooting all of our events. Some angels recorded the audible sermon of the Pastor and wrote down the words of the preaching. They were diligently documenting and shooting the church activities.

The Pastor was very exhausted from battling and casting evil spirits for several weeks. The Pastor could not sleep. His exhaustion prevented him from eating except drinking water. Moreover, his lips were badly blistered and looked very bad. Finally, the Pastor fell onto the floor near the altar from exhaustion. He was not able to get up.

Jesus stood behind the Pastor and stretched out His arms and hands to touch the Pastor's back. As soon as the Lord touched his back, a transparent flashing light entered the body of the Pastor. Two rows of light shaped as small circles continued to enter into the Pastor's body.

From that moment forward, the Pastor's weak sermon energized into a powerful service. The Pastor preached for over four hours. The service turned into a festival.

* Test The Holy Gift Of Prophecy

Jesus said, "Gather the church members who posses the gift of prophecy to teach them. It is the job of the Pastor to teach them." He said that there are more false prophecies these day. Therefore, we have to be more cautious and be fully armed with the Word of God to test the prophecies. He further said that the people who posses prophccy should not be arrogant and speak it carelessly. They must all continue to be humble. They must not go around and boast about their gift to other people.

Most of all, they should pray more often and must not be lazy about reading the Bible. The evil spirits deceive people into speaking false prophesize. Therefore, every time they prophesize, they must prophesize very carefully. I asked the Lord, "Jesus! Jesus! What if I shouted to test you: 'Devil, depart?'" The Lord answered, "It will be all right. It is more important that you are not deceived. You must test it with the Word. Even if it is Me. Do you understand? I replied, "Yes, Lord!"

The Lord spoke to me and said, "Joo-Eun! Today, your mother, Kang, Hyun-Ja barely escaped a bad situation. The third highest ranking devil entered into her body with its subordinates. She must have experienced great pain. Therefore, be very cautious with today's occasion. People who have received the gift of prophecy will have greater trails and temptations. As one gradually opens up with gifts, stronger evil spirits will come and attack! Without knowing the reality of this danger, there are many saints who carelessly ask for the gifts. You must not prophesize imprudently or informally. Understand?" I was determined to be careful.

* Do Not Indiscreetly Use Spiritual Power

Mrs. Kang, Hyun-Ja: After service, I returned home, but the forces of evil spirits had followed me to my home. Then about 50 evil spirits entered my body once again. Due to the great pain, I began to roll and tumble on the floor. In faith I shouted, but it seemed limited as the evil spirits were not so easily thrown out.

In that moment, Jesus said, "You have to cast them out with your faith! Therefore, you are able to go spiritually deeper and have your faith increase." I asked Joo-Eun: "Joo-Eun! Please pray for mother! Quickly!" As Joo-Eun placed her hands on my chest and prayed, the Holy Blazing Fire came out of her body and the fire burned the evil spirits. The Holy Fire instantly turned my body into a fireball. Joo-Eun suddenly moaned and said, "Mother, mother! I cannot bear the Holy Fire exiting out from my body! My arms are hurting so much and my spiritual power is weakening. What should I do? Go and call father — he is writing the book right now."

The Lord then immediately shouted, "No! Pastor Kim is writing the book as I commanded. Since he is concentrating and writing the book, you must not let him use his spiritual power to cast out the evil spirits at this moment. If he utilizes his spiritual power to cast out evil spirits, he will not be able to write the book properly. Joo-Eun, you will have to take your hands off! You will also be in a dangerous situation if your spiritual power is weakened! Saint Hyun-Ja, you must settle this matter with your own faith."

After painfully casting out all the evil spirits, Joo-Eun and I went to the Pastor"s room where he was busy writing the book. With our spiritual eyes, we observed the Pastor moaning and clenching his teeth as he wrote the book. The Pastor"s right arm and back were tattered and torn from the attacks of the evil spirits. There were a few lines shaped like furrows that were torn and scratched. As the Pastor wrote, the unbearable pain brought him tears. Jesus comforted the Pastor as He caressed his back. The Holy Spirit and Jesus stood next to him as they protected him. They became his shield and the evil spirits could not attack him anymore.

After observing the scene, we would be very quiet as the Pastor wrote the book. Our family members would tiptoe as we moved around the house. We even breathed as quietly as possible. To help him concentrate, we became very careful in all matters around the house. Moreover, the Lord had commanded us to be very careful in our ways during this time. We tried not to disturb the Pastor and we had even become nervous when we rested, ate, or slept.

* Repentance

Deaconess Shin, Sung-Kyung: As soon as I began to pray, bright sparks began to flash. Immediately, I began to repent. I usually do not easily tear up, but finally I was flowing in tears. All this time, I had been indolent and lazy. I was repenting entirely for everything. Today, my prayer was especially focused. After some time had passed, my prayer gradually accelerated. Then suddenly, an enormous bright blue object radiated toward me and passed me by. I felt like my prayer was continuously flying toward the sky and into endless space.

March 9th, 2005 (Wednesday)

"I laid me down and slept; I awaked; for the LORD sustained me. I will not be afraid of ten thousands of people, that have set themselves against me round about." (Psalms 3:5-6)

* Electric Power Of The Holy Spirit

Kim, Joo-Eun: During the night service, Jesus spoke. "Today, I will grant you all special power. Therefore, desire to receive it in faith!" I asked, "What are you granting us? The Lord replied, "The electric power of the Holy Spirit!"

I turned and said to the Pastor, "Jesus said that He will grant us Holy Electricity. The Lord will grant the most power to you. The rest of us will receive a little less of the electric power. The Pastor replied, "The word electricity or electric power in the Holy Spirit is not in the Bible. Before the Pastor was able to finish his reply, the Lord interrupted and said, "There is much more power that exists which is not stated in the Bible. There are other unimaginable powers that exist!"

The Lord commanded the members of the Lord's Church to come to the front and to stretch out their hands. The congregation all went to the front of the altar. We formed a circle under the cross which hung above the altar. We began to pray in tongues and longed for grace. With my spiritual eyes, I saw the Holy Spirit's electric current come forth. It first began to flow into the Pastor and instantly, I shouted. "Wow! Impressive!"

Different forms of the Holy Spirit's electricity came down from above. One form came in as lightning. The other form came as a round circle. It continued to spark and shock the Pastor and us. I was reminded of a Sci Fi movie as we were constantly shocked by the electricity. The electricity beamed out various colors including gold. Then other forms of electricity appeared.

As we were constantly shocked by the electricity of the Holy Spirit, we all shouted with one voice. The Holy Spirit and Jesus continued to give us electricity. Not a person from our church refused the electricity. All of us had accepted it. Jesus told us not to be near the Pastor as he received the electricity of the Holy Spirit. The Lord explained that the electricity of the Holy Spirit was so powerful and great that if we accidentally touched it, we may either pass out and or become immobilized. It was dangerous. The Pastor was receiving the electricity in full power since he was a servant of God.

As our faith and spirituality grows deeper and becomes stronger, we will receive greater electric power. The Lord said that there will be a day when the saints of the Lord's Church will be used internationally and on a global scale. I asked the Lord, "Jesus, are there different grades with the electricity of the Holy Spirit? The Lord answered, "Of course, since you are curious and anxious, why don't you test it for yourself? However, do not place your hand on Pastor Kim. Place your hand on your mother, Kang, Hyun-Ja. But touch her lightly.

Cautiously, I lightly grazed the tip of my mother's finger. I began to experience numbness on my hand as it began to go up my arm. With the numbness, I began to feel great pain. The numbness and pain began to spread throughout my body. "Ahhhhhh!" Instantly, I was screaming and the pain did not go away. "Jesus! Jesus! Save me. Help me!" As I was shouting, the Lord said: "Joo-Eun! Do not be so greedy! You are still weak and young and need grow and mature more." When the Lord softly touched my arm and hand, the numbness began to slowly fade away and I soon recovered.

I then realized the electric power of the Holy Spirit. The electric current of the Holy Spirit from my mother was enormously strong. However, the electric current on the Pastor was the most powerful and strongest. My father, the Pastor's, playful nature came forth and he touched all of us and we experienced numbness. We decided to be cautious as the Pastor came near us. As we prayed, we made sure we were not praying near the Pastor.

Pastor Kim, Yong Doo: Whenever the Lord grants us a new type of power, He would make us go deeper in prayer. Moreover, whenever we pray deep in the spirit, we experienced special revelations. Tonight was special. The Holy Spirit granted us fire and electricity during the middle of service. All of the church members had come to the front of the altar to receive the new weapon, the electric power of the Holy Spirit.

We spent about two hours receiving the electric power of the Holy Spirit. An undeserving person like myself received and was baptized by the most powerful and strongest electric power of the Holy Spirit. My heart was beating very rapidly. Perhaps, that was caused by the electric power of the Holy Spirit as it ran through my whole body. Nevertheless, the electricity was flowing deep inside all my organs. The Lord and the Holy Spirit continuously baptized me with the electric power to the point I was able to bear. Before this, we had encountered evil spirits and battled them without any powerful weapons. Now, finally, the Lord had granted us a weapon that we could absolutely use in the spiritual battlefield. The Holy Blazing Fire and Holy Electricity are enormously, unimaginably powerful and can be used as offensive weapons. We will now be able to use them in battle against the demons.

Our bodies were covered with poisonous thorns which were covered with Holy poison The sharp thorns protruded from all our over our bodies. A slight brush of the thorns would instantly burn any demons into ashes. The poison was that powerful. The evil spirits avoided us. However, some of the evil spirits did attempt to penetrate the poisonous thorns. They were the stronger evil spirits and there were many of them. I realized that the groups of evil spirits did not just attack recklessly without a plan. They had organization and an order. I, further, realized they have a hierarchy.

"Finally, my brethren, be strong in the Lord, and in the power of his might. Put on the whole armour of God, that ye may be able to stand against the wiles of the devil. For we wrestle not against flesh and blood, but against principalities, against powers, against the rulers of the darkness of this world, against spiritual wickedness in high places. Wherefore take unto you the whole armour of God, that ye may be able to withstand in the evil day, and having done all, to stand." (Ephesians 6:10-13)

We began praying individually and in unison. We then received the Holy Fire and Electricity for a second time. This time, the Holy Fire and Electricity were much more powerful and stronger. The power of the Holy Fire and Electricity was so great, we were not able to move. After this experience, as we raise our hands high and call upon the name of the Lord, fire and electricity would come upon our bodies. Our bodies would shake as the power manifested onto us.

Whenever we receive fire and electricity, our breathing would sound heavy and we would become a fireball. Our confidence has increased dramatically against the forces of evil. We have become much more powerful.

March 10th, 2005 (Thursday)

Sermon scripture: "Brethren, I count not myself to have apprehended: but this one thing I do, forgetting those things which are behind, and reaching forth unto those things which are before, I press toward the mark for the prize of the high calling of God in Christ Jesus." (Philippians 3:13-14)

* Oh! Pastor Kim, Young Gun

Pastor Kim, Yong-Doo: Sung Min general hospital is located in my neighborhood. Pastor Kim, Young Gun, had evangelized and ministered at this hospital. I had once admitted myself to Sung Min hospital. When I was a patient there, the pastor and I had greeted each other and became acquainted. I had sometimes invited him to my church to give a sermon as a guest speaker.

Pastor Kim, Young Gun once told me a story. He was in his early 60s. He had always evangelized at the hospitals. He was also well known for evangelizing on the streets. One day, he fell ill as his liver swelled. A lot of water filled his liver and stomach. More than that, he also had jaundice, an illness that colors the body yellow. He admitted himself to the hospital while he was evangelizing.

Pastor Kim, Young Gun was once dispatched to the Philippines on a missionary trip by his church. While he was on his mission trip in the Philippines, he had over-exerted himself and worked beyond his physical strengths. The pastor was very stressed by the pressure he received from his church. They wanted results and they called him frequently. "How many people have you evangelized? How many new registrants have you enjoined?" They utilized various tactics to pressure and interrogate him. The pressure and stress eventually overtook him and he had become physically ill. He died during treatment in Korea.

* Hymns That Should Be Sung At A Funeral

Pastor Kim, Young Gun explained the experience when his spirit/soul departed his body. He said when he breathed his last breath he experienced his spirit/soul separate from his physical body. In fact, his spirit/soul looked identical to his physical body. Pastor Kim, Young Gun was able to see the doctor use the defibrillator on his body. The doctors had attempted to resuscitate him several times with the defibrillator. With no result, the doctors confirmed his time of death and had covered his whole body and face with the white linen.

The Pastor's family and relatives had come too late and were informed of his death once they had reached the hospital. On the day of the funeral, the people attending sang hymns. The hymns they sang were slow and the slow rhythm made the day depressing. The funeral was more or less a sad march down to the grave site. The Pastor continued and said that when the people sang the slow songs, his soul weakened. Although he wanted to immediately fly to heaven, he was not able to. He needed the people in the funeral to sing fast, powerful, up-beat hymns. He said that his soul was not gaining any strength and was therefore frustrated and worried. Fortunately, someone recommended hymn 388 and they began to sing in an up-beat rhythm. As soon as the people began singing the fast and powerful hymn, his soul flew at great speed and arrived at the gate of heaven. The Pastor said that the gates of heaven consisted of twelve pearl gates and were a magnificent sight. The Pastor's first impression was amazement: "Literally fantastic!"

As Pastor Kim, Young Gun attempted to enter the pearl gates of heaven, two angels standing guard gave him a stern, frightening look. The Pastor became very frightened and his heart was filled with fear. The two angels had a large sword at their side. They were very tall and he could not properly view all of them with one glance.

The angels asked the Pastor: "How dare you walk near the gate? Who are you? What is your title and what did you do when you were on earth?" The Pastor answered, "I had just died from an illness; my liver swelled. I was a Pastor and I worked as a missionary." The angels demanded a ticket. "Very well, present your ticket of permission to enter heaven. Now!" I replied in shock. "What! You need a permission ticket to enter heaven? I had never heard of such thing! I do not have one." One of the angels immediately replied: "What! What are you saying? How dare you walk toward the gate without a permission ticket!" As the angel rebuked me, the other angel kicked me like I was a soccer ball. In that moment, the Pastor thought he was kicked very far off. Then the same angel who had kicked him caught up to him and kicked him once more for a second time and even farther away.

The Pastor was suddenly kicked toward hell and was dangling at the edge of a cliff. The Pastor was able to observe the miserable sights of hell. As the Pastor dangled off the edge of the cliff, he pleaded for someone to save him. Then the angel pointed and said, "Look at those souls! Look very closely at those souls going to hell! All of those souls attended church and lived a faithful life but the errors of their Pastor's teaching led them to hell! I am showing you this scene because you are also a Pastor who led a ministry. You cannot be forgiven for you have committed the same atrocity. They did not keep Sundays holy and did not properly keep their faith. They mocked God and believed according to what they wanted to believe and based their faith on what was in their minds."

Within the moment Pastor Kim was about to be thrown in hell, two souls immediately came and earnestly grabbed hold of him. The Pastor found out later that the two souls were his relatives who were prayer warriors. Due to their earnest pleadings, the Lord had granted the Pastor an extension of seven more years to live. The Pastor received special grace. He had been given another chance and had escaped from being thrown into hell.

The Pastor came back down to earth to reunite with his dead body. When he came back, his relatives were still singing hymns. The songs they were singing were once again slow and sad. They sounded like farewell songs, as though, a couple or friends were parting forever. The Pastor was very upset over the songs that were being sung. Whenever believers sleep and go to heaven, the people at the funeral should be celebrating with fast, joyous, enliven, and victorious hymns. We as believers must engrave this into our hearts.

He had experienced a supernatural event. With the power of God, the Pastor had come back alive. Now, this is the seventh year and because of exhaustion and illness, he had relapsed once more. His liver had swelled up and the Pastor had to be admitted to intensive care. Pastor Kim, Young Gun earnestly appealed, "Pastor Kim, Yong-Doo, I was very proud of myself. Until now, I thought I had evangelized properly throughout my life and in faith. I later realized that I had done it all with my strength and passion instead with the guidance and help of the Holy Spirit. Please Pastor Kim, Yong-Doo, you must seek help from the Holy Spirit in every case. I want you to lead your ministry with the help and strength of the Holy Spirit." Pastor Kim, Young Gun then asked me to sing many hymns that are powerful and strengthening. Joo-Eun, Sister Baek, Bong-Nyu, my wife, and I gathered around Pastor Kim, Young Gun. The Lord, Jesus, accompanied us as well. Jesus, the Holy Spirit, and the guardian angels watched and prepared to take the Pastor to heaven.

Today is Thursday and the Lord announced that He was going to take Pastor Kim, Young Gun to heaven soon. When Joo-Eun and Sister Baek, Bong- Nyu glanced up to heaven, the home of Pastor Kim was almost finished. The last thing was for the Pastor's soul to arrive in heaven. His home was waiting. Pastor Kim, Young

Gun and his wife were very joyous once they heard of that news.

* If I Die, I Want To Die During Preaching A Sermon On The Platform

There are many pastors, including myself, who wish on a certain issue. I had been curious on how the Lord may respond and what His thoughts would be with this certain issue. "My beloved, Jesus! There are many pastors in Korea and many are especially filled with grace. They often say that when they go they would like their last moment to be on the altar during the middle of their sermon. I also wish for that. Now, Pastor Kim, Young Gun has fallen ill due to his liver swelling as a result of over-exhaustion and exertion. He had not taken care of himself very well physically. What are your thoughts on that, Lord?"

The Lord began to explain in regard to this matter using Pastor Kim, Young Gun as an example. "It is truly regrettable. It is foolish to think and act this way! Pastor Kim, Young Gun is a servant I truly esteem. But for the sake of the gospel, he went through fire and water not taking care of his health. Therefore, he had become ill. Father God, the Holy Spirit, and I are in agreement with this view. From your perception, it may appear as a blessing. It may seem faithful to collapse from exhaustion or exertion during the middle of evangelizing or preaching — perhaps even dying during evangelizing or preaching. However, that is not everything! Being faithful with all of your strength is very important, but not at the expense of your physical bodies. You must take care of your bodies in order to continue and serve me for a long time. Your body is given to you by Father God. There is a time to rest and a proper amount is needed and required.

"It is not wise for one to do my work with only absolute enthusiasm. One must do the work with wisdom. Pastor Kim, Young Gun was only in his early 60s and he could have continued my work for a longer period. He was very foolish and not very wise. He did not realize how I esteemed him! However, it is now too late."

I thought it would have been nice if Jesus would have healed him. However, it appears that the Lord had decided to take him home to heaven. The Lord made it absolutely clear that doing His work in faithfulness and with all of our being was very important. Moreover, taking care of our physical bodies continuously was equally important. The majority truly do think that it is certainly good faith if we go through fire and water for the Lord's concern, but that is not everything, although, it is important.

The Lord said, "The physical body of Pastor Kim, Young Gun had become sick and exhausted. It is his time to rest now." The Lord then looked at me and said, "Pastor Kim, Yong-Doo, you must also listen carefully! Do you understand? In order to serve for a lengthy period, you must steadily take care of your health." I replied, "Amen."

Joo-Eun had a vision of God"s throne. Father God also said, "My beloved servant! Why did you over work yourself to have your body come to that stage?" As Father spoke, He had compassion on him. He then commanded the angels. "Prepare to welcome Pastor Kim, Young Gun." As Pastor Kim, Young Gun laid in bed, Jesus caressed him and said with comforting words, "You will enter heaven very soon. In heaven, all the souls and angels are preparing a great event to welcome you. Although it will be a bit difficult for a moment, I expect you to endure it."

As Pastor Kim, Young Gun listened to the conversation, his face brightened up. Pastor Kim, Young Gun's guardian angel had three pairs of wings. He had a home that was awaiting him in heaven. The house was as tall as the skies of heaven. Inside the home, the angels were busy moving about, preparing for his arrival. Joo-Eun wanted to know when Pastor Kim, Young Gun was going to heaven and asked Jesus. The Lord said that He would take him to heaven after two days.

I meticulously explained some of the revelations that were happening in our church. The Pastor answered with a surprised look. "What! When I had visited your church to speak, none of those experiences or revelations were occurring. Now your church is experiencing great revelations." I answered him, stating that it was all due to the Lord's grace. I continued and asked Pastor Kim, Young Gun: "Pastor Kim! Before you leave the earth, I would like to share Holy Communion with you for the last time." Pastor Kim delightfully accepted. The Lord then spoke through Joo-Eun: "In a little while, you will enter heaven. Let us then celebrate." I obeyed and said, "Amen!"

Chapter 4
The Secret Room

March 12th, 2005 (Saturday)

Sermon scripture: "Two are better than one; because they have a good reward for their labour. For if they fall, the one will lift up his fellow: but woe to him that is alone when he falleth; for he hath not another to help him up. Again, if two lie together, then they have heat: but how can one be warm alone? And if one prevail against him, two shall withstand him; and a threefold cord is not quickly broken." (Ecclesiastes 4:9-12)

* Pastor Kim, Young Gun In Heaven

Pastor Kim, Yong-Doo: Sung Min hospital had contacted and notified me that Pastor Kim, Young Gun had just died. It rained heavily all throughout the day. By late afternoon, the sky was covered with black clouds. Lightning filled the sky as the sounds of thunder shook the throughout the sky. God spoke to Joo-Eun in an audible voice. "My heart is sorrowful because the life of my beloved and esteemed servant has ended! Do not be afraid to document it. You should document these types of events in the book. Rain represents my tears. I desire all to realize it!"

Jesus standing next to me spoke gently. "Many saints and pastors cannot be used because they are lazy and self-indulging. Then there are some who physically over-exert themselves and as a result become ill. This is also a problem! Moreover, unnecessarily idolizing one"s physical body is also a big sin."

The Lord explained how saints enjoyed recreational sport activities. "They indulge in their recreations too much. Those activities become more important than Me. I am very sorrowful about it."

As a matter of fact, we entangle ourselves with various kinds of business and/or recreational activities and give the excuse that we are too busy for the Lord. We then often forget the Lord. Rather than relying on the Kingdom of God, we rest on our current physical world. As a result, we miss hearing the voice of God. Slowly and gradually, we change and follow the life that is irrelevant to the Lord.

Today, the members of the Lord's church live a life totally different from they had before. Our faith has totally changed spiritually. Since we now know the Lord's will, the church members, my family, and I cannot live in complacency or indolence to the Lord anymore. We now always put the Lord and His business first.

* King Snake In The Form Of A Spring Coil

Sister Baek, Bong-Nyu: While I was in fervent prayer, the Lord showed me a vision. In the vision, many small snakes had covered the earth. I was frightened and felt like vomiting from the revolting appearance of the snakes. The small snakes had formed a coil with their bodies to form a line. The line continued endlessly. From a distance, the line of small snakes appeared to be one large snake. The line connected to hell. As I quickly glanced at the small snakes, they all formed to look like a spring.

As the snakes were coiled around the earth, small insects that looked like maggots came out from the bodies of the snakes. The insects attached themselves to the people and dragged them to hell through the pathway of the line. The maggots had hundreds of tiny legs which attached to the peoples's bodies and they did not fall off. The Lord gave an explanation to the nature of these people. These were the souls that did not believe in Jesus. The Lord had given these people countless opportunities to believe unto Him but did not.

* Meeting Pastor Kim, Young Gun In Heaven

Lee, Haak-Sung: After the hospital had notified us of the Pastor's passing, I thought to myself. 'Tonight, it is my determination to meet Pastor Kim, Young Gun in heaven!' We began to pray once the pastor's sermon had concluded. When I began to pray, I entered heaven with the Lord. I was very excited and in ecstasy as I thought about meeting Pastor Kim, Young Gun. I asked the Lord, "Jesus! Please allow me to meet Pastor Kim, Young Gun. He had died today but I already miss him." Jesus said, "He has just arrived and is very busy looking and venturing all around the places in heaven." As I tilted my head down, I asked again. "Lord, can you please lead me to him?" The Lord replied, "Very well."

The Lord pointed to the flower garden. "Look over there." As the Lord pointed, I looked toward the flower garden and saw Pastor Kim, Young Gun running around like a little boy. I ran toward the pastor and shouted. "Pastor! Pastor! Pastor Kim, Young Gun. It is I, Haak-Sung."

But the pastor replied, "Who? I don"t think I recognize you." I in turn said, "I attend the Lord's Church and my name is Lee, Haak-Sung. I met you once when you were in the hospital. My pastor is Kim, Yong-Doo." He then recognized me and said, "Yes, yes! That is right! The Lord's Church is very well known in heaven. I had not known how well known the Lord's Church was on earth, but I had now realized it after I had arrived here. It is a great church. Give my best regards to Pastor Kim, Yong-Doo! Tell him that I would like to meet him in the near future. Therefore, I hope his spiritual eyes are opened as soon as possible." As I watched, Pastor Kim, Young Gun rejoiced like a little boy. He ran all over the place and was busy sight-seeing.

Sister Baek, Bong-Nyu: After I had witnessed the gruesome scenes in hell, I went to heaven. I then met Pastor Kim, Young Gun. He had just passed away today but he was now looking like a handsome young man.

As soon as the pastor saw me, he clapped and said, "Welcome! Sister Baek, Bong-Nyu. I have heard about you and your church many times. I am in so much joy that I do not know what to do! After I had passed, you sang a lot of great hymns and I was very thankful. Earnestly walk in faith at the Lord's Church. Oh, and I forgot to recommend Pastor Kim, Yong-Doo as my successor to senior Pastor. I regret greatly in forgetting my last wishes while I was in the hospital. After I had arrived in heaven and observed the Lord's Church from heaven's giant screen, I had realized the Lord's Church was very well known.

The pastor and I said our farewells to each other and I returned to the Lord's Church. I then began to pray. I told Pastor Kim, Yong-Doo about my encounter with Pastor Kim, Yong Gun in heaven.

March 13th, 2005 (Sunday)

Sermon scripture: "For I desire mercy, not sacrifice; and the knowledge of God more than burnt offerings. But they like men have transgressed the covenant: there have they dealt treacherously against me." (Hosea 6:6-7)

* About Dog Meat

Pastor Kim, Yong-Doo: "Jesus! Many people in Korea enjoy eating soup composed of dog meat. I have also eaten dog meat many times. Some people have stated that if people eat dog meat, they will become spiritually turbid and inebriated. Lord, what is your answer to this?"

The Lord kept silent for quite some time. I was very curious. The Jesus said, "You cannot eat everything, even if those foods may be good for your body. Dog meat is not spiritually beneficial. Therefore, try not to eat any dog meat. Dogs are animals that perform lewd and unclean acts. Eating them will make you spiritually weak."

* Keeping Sunday Holy, Do Not Spend Money On Sundays

I decided to ask the Lord about Sundays, the Sabbath day: how we should keep it Holy and if we are to spend any money on Sundays. I wondered how He thought about it. "Lord! Currently, I see many churches and saints not keeping Sundays holy. Sundays are utilized by families to eat out, as a day for recreation, and to spend time on their hobbies. They say that if those things are done for the sake of the gospel, it is justified. Their conviction of keeping Sundays holy is lackadaisical at best. Moreover, their faith has no convictions to God's Word. The servants of God are not emphasizing the importance of this subject in their sermons. Furthermore, Sunday evening services are gradually decreasing and being eliminated.

Most only have day services. Please give me your thoughts on this subject."

As soon as I asked, the Lord became quickly angry. His expression changed and His anger showed on His face. The Lord wanted me to reference and document scripture: scripture that described kindling a fire to those who do not keep Sunday holy.

"But if ye will not hearken unto me to hallow the Sabbath day, and not to bear a burden, even entering in at the gates of Jerusalem on the Sabbath day; then will I kindle a fire in the gates of thereof, and it shall devour the palaces of Jerusalem and it shall not be quenched." (Jeremiah 17:27)

"If thou turn away thy foot from the Sabbath, from doing thy pleasure on my holy day; and call a Sabbath a delight, the Holy of the Lord, honorable and shall honour Him, not doing thine own ways, nor finding thine own pleasure, nor speaking thine own words. Then shall thou delight thyself in the Lord, and I will cause thee to ride upon the high places of the earth, and feed thee with the heritage of Jacob thy father: for the mouth of the Lord hath spoken it" (Isaiah 58:13-14)

"For the Son of man is Lord even of the Sabbath day" (Matthew 12:8) "Wherefore it is lawful to do well on the Sabbath days." (Matthew 12:12)

The Lord had commanded us to keep Sundays Holy in every way. He rebuked watching television, dining out with family, and other secular activities. Furthermore, the Lord did not permit Christians to run any business of any kind for profit on Sundays. He also did not approve Saints to do any shopping on Sundays.

As a matter of fact, only a few saints barely made it to heaven that did not keep Sundays properly. And on the contrary, there were an over flowing number of saints who were in hell for not keeping

Sunday holy. The saints in hell were shouting in anguish. They were experiencing countless degrees of torment.

The Lord commanded: "Look at those souls! Those souls did not consider my day with much relevance. They had made my day unclean. Look very closely." The church congregation and I had witnessed a shocking scene. We were in total shock. After witnessing the scene, I concentrated on repenting of not keeping Sundays Holy in every way.

We need to adjust our concept of Sundays. There are numerous saints who think that spending money on Sundays is justified if it is for the sake of the gospel. With that thought, they spend money on Sundays.

"And he said unto them, the Sabbath was made for man, and not man for the Sabbath: Therefore the Son of Man is Lord also of the Sabbath." (Mark 2:27-28)

If we simply justify spending money for the sake of the gospel and for the sake of people, then everybody will validate with their own reasoning to spend money on Sundays. Eventually, they will continuously create more special cases or reasons to spend money. Within time, people will create their own excuses to spend money on Sundays.

The Lord had clearly clarified the reality of the church's deception

The Lord stated. "People obfuscate, misuse, and abuse the commandment of Sunday for the sake of the gospel. They do it consistently. Do not spend money on Sundays! Once men have decided to do what is in their hearts, they present their reasons or justifications to break the commandment at any cost." The Lord looked very serious. His majesty overflowed. His seriousness and majesty vividly touched me.

Moreover, on Sundays, Jesus did not want us to spend any money on the coffee machine before or after a meal in church. The Lord desired us to raise money for missions and missionaries on weekdays and not on Sundays. The Lord told me to document this problem. Currently, the people throughout the churches cry out for revival and reformation but the ministers and church congregations must first be changed. They must fearfully repent. They do not properly teach or proclaim keeping Sunday Holy. In fact, they treat this matter with negligence. The Lord had given a stern warning.

Any kind of events held in the house of God must be free of charge. Many churches today sell meal tickets since they have numerous attendants. Purchasing meal tickets is not keeping Sundays Holy. The Lord meticulously showed me how Korean churches and the saints therein are not approved by our Holy God — just by not keeping Sunday Holy.

The Lord also wanted the church to feed any guest speakers at either the Pastor's house or a saint's house if the special event is held on Sundays. The Lord did not want the church to take the guest speaker out to a restaurant on Sundays. If the church had a kitchen, the guests could be fed there. The Lord ended His admonition by stating that He forbade us to spend money on Sundays.

I would like to disclose an event a church member experienced in church. My son, Joseph, evangelized to his friend, Oh, Seung-Young. He had invited him to our church. While we laid our hands on him and prayed, his spiritual eyes opened. He was not aware or ignorant about keeping Sundays holy. Out of habit, he continued to casually buy bubble gum on Sundays. Then one evening on Sunday during church service, he was brought before the throne of God.

God immediately said, "Seung-Young! Why have you made my day unclean? Why have you not kept Sunday holy? My heart is woeful and breaks." God then laid him on his stomach and spanked him six times. Seung-Young felt the tingles on his butt as he laid on his stomach. Then God ordered him to do push ups.

While Seung-Young was being punished, the other church saints were praying. prophecies- Young was also praying in his physical state. While we all prayed, Seung-Young, out of the blue, gasped. I asked, "What are you doing? Shouldn't you be praying?" Seung-Young shouted, "Pastor! I bought a bubble gum this afternoon and now God is punishing me for breaking His commandment of keeping Sunday holy. I am being punished right now."

After being disciplined, Father God said, "Seung-Young! Since my heart is woeful, cheer me up now. Appease and gratify Me!" Seung-Young stopped his push ups and began dancing in a humorous way before the Lord. God became very delighted.

God commanded Seung-Young never to purchase any gum or snacks on Sunday. God proclaimed that Sundays are Holy and must be kept holy. Seung-Young continuously said, "Amen!" He obeyed God.

As a Pastor, I had never properly taught my congregation about keeping Sundays Holy. I, myself, have not kept Sundays Holy as well. Therefore, I repented. Now with a fearful and trembling heart, I wholly keep Sundays Holy. My family and I, including the church congregation, avoid going out for personal pleasures of any kind. Now on Sundays, we gather together in church to have service and evangelize. We gain rest from it.

March 15th, 2005 (Tuesday)

Sermon scripture: "Therefore also now, saith the Lord, turn ye even to me with all your heart, and with fasting, and with weeping, and with mourning. And rend your heart, and not your garments, and turn unto the Lord your God: for He is gracious and merciful, slow to anger, and of great kindness, and repenteth him of the evil." (Joel 2:12-13)

* The Salvation Of My Family And Their Relatives

Pastor Kim, Yong-Doo: My wife, Joseph, Joo-Eun and I sat together in a circle. It has been a long time since the four of us spent quality time together. Jesus sat in the center of us. The Holy Spirit surrounded our family with a protective light. Within the protective light, we were able to converse with the Lord and the Holy Spirit. We talked about the salvation of our relatives. We discussed about the spiritual state of our relatives. We wondered if they were to die right now, would they be saved? Basically, the question was if their spiritual state was acceptable. My family and I had a deep conversation on this matter.

Outside the protective light stood a group of angels from heaven with our guardian angels. Both groups of angels were confronting the dark forces of Satan. The evil spirits could not hear the conversation that was being discussed within the protective light. In fact, the evil spirits could not come close to the light.

Joo-Eun was the first to ask the big question to Jesus. "My beloved Jesus! As you already know, we are the pastoral family. Are we all saved? Please let my father, mother, my big brother, and I all enter heaven, no matter what! Does our current faith qualify us to enter heaven?" The Lord answered, "Of course! Your faiths are good enough to enter heaven. But do not become arrogant; always be humble! Furthermore, do more of my works — do you understand?" All of our family members said in one voice, "Amen!"

The problem began to arise from the next question. The answer to that question made me very distressful. I was very curious about the salvation of our relatives. How many of them were saved? I was curious about the Lord's perspective with my brothers. "Jesus, Jesus! My mother, my older brother's family, my older sister's family, nephews, and nieces all attend their own churches. I would like to request an answer from you, Lord. Please teach and provide an answer that is accurate and definite. If you are able to answer, I can visit them in person to encourage all of them, right?" As I seriously asked, the Lord kept silent for a while.

After some time had passed, the Lord finally spoke: "Pastor Kim! I know this may be hard to accept and heartbreaking, but you must listen to Me carefully. Regrettably, within your family, there are only about three or four souls who have faith which qualifies to enter heaven." Surprised, I replied. "What? Lord! What are you saying? My relatives have studied and been trained in discipleship. In fact, each morning, some of them are studying and meditating on God's word daily. They have committed their life in studying the Word with fervent faith. They appear to be very faithful. I cannot believe what I have just heard. Lord! Please check their hearts one more time and give me the answer again. Please Lord!"

* A Defiant Attitude Toward The Lord

Jesus said, "There is a deeper problem beyond your understanding. Pastor Kim, listen very carefully to what I have to say now. I do not see one's outward appearance like you do. I see their hearts. I see the inside. I know every inch of one's thought and heart. No one can ever deceive Me, the Father, or the Holy Spirit. Do not concern yourself with how many are going to Heaven! Your brothers and relatives believe they are serving Me, but they do not have love and they lack sincerity in their hearts. If they later repent, they will be able to enter heaven. But they will have to repent sincerely and live by My Words. Nevertheless, they continue to live a life with superficial faith and do not tremble at My Word! They have many areas to repent remorsefully." (Isaiah 66:2)

Until this moment, from my perspective, my brothers and relatives seemed so faithful. I never doubted their faith. In fact, I was very confident about their faith. However, there is a big difference between my perspective and the Lord's.

I have a mother with four brothers and one sister. I was number four among my brothers. My other three brothers are pastors as well. The rest of my relatives are part of the laity in other churches. All of them put in their best efforts to serve their churches.

If I include all of my nephews and nieces, the total number of my relatives would equal to about twenty. But there are only 3 or 4 saved? How on earth can the Lord say that? How can I accept this reality? I was very agitated on the inside. Within a short time, my bad temper exploded.

I began to rudely speak to Jesus. "Lord! If that is the case, how many people do you think can enter heaven? Who wouldn't want to go to heaven? If someone lived in assurance and belief of their faith, but did not receive salvation after death, wouldn't they think that would be unfair? I just cannot possibly understand. My brothers, nieces, and nephews never drank or smoked. They all attend church service every Sunday. Moreover, they serve the church and volunteer and support the operational functions of the church. They are hoping and cherishing the day they go to heaven. What do they have to do more besides what they are currently doing? Lord! From today, I will stop writing the book. I will not write the book." Stubbornly, I was in defiance. For several days, I did not continue with the book.

The Lord spoke to me with a resonant, fearful voice. "Pastor Kim! Do not stop writing the book! You cannot stop! If you resist, you will give victory to the devil. Quickly, grab your pen and began writing. You have to expose the identities of the devils!" As the Lord spoke, He tried to calm me. However, I was unbearably shocked by the fact that my brothers were not going to heaven. For several days, my heart was troubled and severely beating. I resented this fact and I became a nervous wreck.

I was in defiance to the Lord almost every day. With my finite mind, I could not understand. I was behaving irrationally and evil began to slowly creep into my heart. Salvation was not something I could negotiate with the Lord. But I was determined to make a deal with the Lord. Although, I knew it was impossible, I thought about using the book as leverage to negotiate for the salvation of my relatives. I was going to stop the book if the Lord did not give me the answers I desired. Do my brothers know I am in such torment?

"For I desire mercy, and not sacrifice; and the knowledge of God more than burnt offerings." (Hosea 6:6)

"Then shall we know, if we follow on to know the Lord: his going forth is prepared as the morning; and he shall come unto us as the rain, as the latter and former rain unto the earth." (Hosea 6:3)

"Sow to yourselves in righteousness, reap in mercy; break up your fallow ground: for it is time to seek the Lord, till He come and rain righteousness upon you. Ye have plowed wickedness, ye have reaped iniquity; ye have eaten the fruit of lies: because thou didst trust in thy way, in the multitude of thy mighty men."
(Hosea 10:12-13)

The Word of Jesus continued. "Many churches throughout the world, including the churches in Korea, are overflowing with

Pharisees who are proud and satisfied with their own righteousness. The hearts are content with their own righteousness but I want broken hearts."

"The Lord is close to the brokenhearted and saves those who are crushed in spirit" (Psalms 34:18).

During the middle of the book, I resisted and stopped writing. At that time, my anxiety and nerves had reached a climatic point. I could no longer bear the thought and pain of my little brother not entering heaven. I used to watch and babysit him. I could remember the delightful memories of the cute baby. And to top it off, even my mother? My mother as well? The Lord said that many Christians are more concerned about material blessings than seeking the spiritual blessing and life. The desires of their physical sight and needs have become their way of life. Regretfully, the Lord said, "The saints have become greedy for material blessings." That was His diagnosis of the church.

The Lord then spoke about the ministers. I was shocked when He described the problems. The problems were most severe. I had made up my mind to document it at a later time. I wanted to give some time in prayer about it. Before anything else, my family's salvation was the most important matter. Although my brothers and their family members were living a life of faith, the Lord had said that their current spiritual conditions made it difficult for them to enter heaven. Therefore, I will resist writing this book and be defiant to the end. I was even prepared to receive the Lord's punishment. Even if that punishment was severe enough to be death, I was determined.

I began to protest as I shouted to the Lord. Joseph and Joo-Eun sat next to me as my children attempted to deliver the Lord's message to me. As my children delivered the message to me, they also attempted to calm me down. I said, "Lord! How is that right? Why are you doing it this way? I cannot agree with you. I cannot accept it. How is this able to be true? Among my brothers and their families, how can there only be a few of them going to heaven? Why such a small number?" My egregious question made the Lord perplexed and sad. I was not concerned about the Lord's feeling and I continued to press the Lord with my questions aggressively. "I know that they fervently study the Bible every Sunday. Moreover, on Sundays, they do not spend any money for their own pleasures or desires. They spend Sunday in devotion. Do not they live their lives as the Bible requires? So are you saying that the word from the Bible is in error? What are the reasons for them not being able to enter heaven?"

While I was in defiance and as I continued to do so for several days, the Lord had finally decided to help me understand and realize what I needed to know. The Lord made me instantly faint. As my body was in a state of unconsciousness, He began to work and show me the answers in which I could understand with clarity.

* Pastor Kim Finally Stands In Front Of God's Throne

The Lord Himself took me to heaven. Jesus and I walked toward the throne where Father God was sitting. I had no idea how or what procedure, stages, route, or process I had to go through when I had arrived in heaven. Without knowing how I got there, I was in heaven. Although my physical body was in a deep sleep, my spirit had all my senses and I was seeing things as though I would in my physical state.

I was located in a place where an enormous light shined unimaginably bright. I realized I was standing in front of Father. It was indescribable; I would never measure His mightiness.
His voice was very deep, and it echoed around my body like a wind. The voice of Father God was the voice I had always eagerly longed to hear.

As I stood in front of Him, I was but only a helpless sinner. I had clearly and finally found the entity of myself. My whole body trembled. God's holiness and majesty unceasingly poured down in an array of colors. Father God said, "Oh! My beloved Pastor Kim, You came! You must be tired from coming all the way here!" When Father spoke, I became overwhelmed with extreme shock and unspeakable emotions.

I had only documented other people's experiences through their testimonies. I had felt the word of God through reading, speaking, or listening. But now, I was actually looking at God in person and my soul was in much happiness and joy.

I felt as though I was a less-than-simple being who was not even worth dust. I was standing in front of Father, totally stripped and broken. I was a wounded creation. Standing in front of Father God, I felt like a sinner who was awaiting a death sentence. My rude behaviors of praying and defiance disappeared completely — which was so evident shortly ago to the Son of God, Jesus. Now, I was in a situation that waited for God's discipline and compassion.

* The Temple Of Heaven

God's enormous hand came down from above to pat my head. His very deep, wavering voice continued. As I stood in front of God's throne, I witnessed the judgments made to the multitudes of souls. They were either destined to heaven or hell. I also witnessed spiritual beings at the front of Father God's throne give respectful bows and worship as they played trumpets. The spiritual beings were so numerous, I was unable to count their number.
I also witnessed a special sight. As I stood in the front of Father God's throne, toward the left side of His seat, I held Jesus's hand and viewed a scene that seemed to be an reenactment of Job 1:6, 2:1-3.

Suddenly, I felt a cold energy around me when an ugly, heinous, wild-looking being appeared in front of God"s throne. This place was flowing with God's majesty, holiness, and glory. However, when the ugly being appeared, I was able to smell stench and feel evil energy.

The evil kowtowed continuously toward Father. How this evil being unceasingly grumbled and complained against something. At that moment, I instantly knew: 'This being is the one that has led multitudes of souls astray and had seduced the whole world — Satan!'

I do not know how Satan was able to obtain an audience in front of the throne of God. What was his procedure or right? Perhaps, Job 1:6 is appropriate Biblical scripture for this situation. "Now there was a day when the sons of God came to present themselves before the Lord, and Satan came also among them." Satan appeared as a hybrid of a human and monster, perhaps, because he was cursed. Satan had a face of a deformed animal. On his face spouted many various horns and hideous tumors. His mouth resembled that of a frog. Satan's body was covered with repulsive, needle-shaped hairs. I also noticed a thick tail and it reminded me of a monkey's long tail. He gestured annoyingly with his hands and feet. Moreover, he used a variety of body movements to express his argument with God. My body shivered as I saw his sharp fingernails and toenails. They looked like they were from a wild beast.

Satan was attempting to obtain some type of special permission from Father God. Although Father God and Jesus were beside me, I was still very nervous. I was so nervous I thought I was going to have a panic attack. The Lord noticed my anxiety and tightly held my hand to comfort me. "Do not worry." Before the authority and power of Father God, Satan abased himself. With Satan's head bowing down, he glanced at me with an evil look. He was gnashing his teeth in anger and I was able to hear what he was thinking: "Pastor Kim! Just wait and see! I will tear you down.

How dare you expose my identity? I will not forgive you, your church or your family." I almost felt parallelized as I heard his threats.

As I began to shake in fear, Father God rebuked Satan with an enormous voice. The devil instantly expelled himself. When Father God vociferated at Satan, the skies of heaven vibrated like lightning and thunder. Father God's voice resonated throughout heaven, space, and to the earth.

This brief event made me shiver in fear of Father God. The souls waiting for judgment by Father God who were in front of the throne all held their heads down in great fear. Around this time, I began to hear from Father God. His voice was much deeper than a baritone sound; it was soft and wavering. Once I heard Father's voice, the sense of fear and apprehension instantly disappeared. My body ceased to shiver as well. A gentle energy blanketed my body as I experienced His compassion. I was now in complete tranquility.

Father God spoke: "Pastor Kim, Yong-Doo, shepherd of the Lord's Church, since you did not believe, I had commanded that you be here. I will clearly show you, so that you may believe and understand. Look very carefully! Now, take him to the secret room of the sanctuary! I have something special to show you. I will personally explain it to you!" With the Father's command, the Lord led me to the heavenly sanctuary where the secret room was located.

* The Secret Room

In heaven, no souls are allowed to approach the secret room. I am not able to disclose what I had witnessed in the secret room. Initially, I had no idea there was a heavenly sanctuary or a secret room. I mistakenly blurted out and spoke of this place to my children. For several months, I diligently requested permission to document and mention this secret room. The secret room is also used as a meeting room. This room is used especially for meetings with Trinity God and Moses. The Lord had explained that no other souls have entered here except for Moses. He said that this area was a restricted area. "No one has ever entered here except Moses. And now you are the only other person allowed, Pastor Kim." As I entered the room, Moses was already waiting.

Jesus and Moses went to the corner of the room and sat on bright shinning, golden chairs. They faced each other and began to converse with one another. Between the Lord and Moses sat the Ark of the Covenant. The Ark looked just like as it was described in the five books of Moses. The Ark was made out of gold and it appeared as though it looked the same as it was when it was first built.

As I looked around the room, it didn't appear very large. However, the room was decorated with many different precious and rare stones. The room was filled with jewels, gold, and diamonds. Unexpectedly, the floor was laid out with square-shaped tile marble which looked similar to the ones I see on earth. A cross was stenciled in center of the marble tiled floor. On one side of the room, the wall was transparent. As I looked into the transparent wall, I was able to see the vigorous Blazing Holy Fire. I could not see the end of the room where the Blazing Holy Fire burned. The other side of the room must have been quite a distance.

* God Makes A Special Appearance

As Jesus and Moses were talking to one another, I quietly walked around the marble floor. Jesus and Moses occasionally glanced at me as they seemed to have a pleasant, enjoyable conversation. My mind raced and I had all kinds of questions. 'How did I come to this point? What will take place here?' I was very curious.

I was defiant to God because of the question of my beloved mother and brothers's salvation. This is why I am here. I must prevent my family from going to hell, whether I use the correct methods or perhaps somehow cheat. They must go to heaven with me. Why did the Lord states that only a couple of them will enter heaven? What would the reason be for that statement? As my mind raced and all these questions and thoughts entered my mind, an enormous, shining light shone down on me. I could not lift my head up as the light shined upon me. Father God said, "Pastor Kim, look at me." With His command, I lifted my head up to look at Him. Father was within the glorious beam. He toned down His light so that I was able to see His legs and feet. As a matter of fact, I was not able to see more than His legs and feet.

"And the Lord spoke unto you out of the midst of the fire: ye heard the voice of the words, but saw no similitude; only ye heard a voice." (Deuteronomy 4:12)

"Who only hath immortality, dwelling in the light which no man can approach unto; whom no man hath seen, nor can see: to whom be honor and power everlasting. Amen" (1 Timothy 6:16)

"No man hath seen God at any time, the only begotten Son, which is in the bosom of the Father, he hath declared Him" (John 1:18)

"And he said, Thou canst not see my face: for there shall no man see me, and live" (Exodus 33:20)
"Not that any man hath seen the Father, have he which is of God, he hath seen the Father." (John 6:46)

As you have read the above Biblical scriptures, we can understand that no one can see all of Father God. Even if I had asked persistently, it would not make a difference; I would not be able to see all of Father God. I know what I document may bring enormous criticism, but I must still document what I have seen and heard. It is granted by God's grace and compassion. I cannot really say I saw all of Father God. I only saw what He allowed me to see of Himself.

God is the God of ages. He lives throughout eternity. Sinners like myself dare not approach near Him. However, I can see and feel Father God and I know I have since scripture tells me that if I have seen Jesus, I have seen Father God.

I lifted my head to see if Father God sitting on His throne might be Jesus. But Jesus was sitting at the corner of the room still having a pleasant conversation with Moses. Father God, knowing my thoughts spoke: "I am Jehovah!" He then laughed.
Father continued to speak in a benevolent voice. "My beloved servant! Lie on your face!" I laid in the center of the room where the cross was stenciled to the marble floor. As I laid, I spread my arms out and shaped my body as a cross.

God's large hand came toward me and He laid His hand on my back and prayed. "I am giving you power! You will possess the power of fire. You and your flock will perform a fire ministry."

As soon as Father prayed over me, I began to tumble on the floor. I was burning up. With the sensation of heat, I also became emotional and sadness overwhelmed me. I loudly shouted, "Father God! You have poured all of your powers unto me. What if the power corrupts me with pride and I use it incorrectly? Please, help me so that I may not become corrupt or prideful. Father God, you know my past, present, and future. Right? What is my future like? Please show me! Please help me with this power. I do not want to become corrupt. I want to enter heaven." As Father God observed me pleading, He said. "Very well, I will be with you."

I was not satisfied with His answer. With this opportunity, I persistently cried out for my family's salvation. I began to cry out with all my strength and tumble onto the marble floor. Due to my actions, in an instant, the mood of the secret room partially filled with sad energy. I unceasingly cried with repentance and with prayers of supplication. "Father God! Please, I ask of you. What is the result of my mother and brothers" salvation? Many of my family members are believing and serving you. Why are only three or four saved? Why is that? What about my little brother? If he is not saved, the alternative is hell….Please save him. Please! I raised him up as my own. Lord! Father God!" I continuously cried out. As I cried, I tumbled and rolled on the floor.

As I continued to roll, tumble, and cried out, Father began to comfort me. "Very well! Very well! Pastor Kim! I know why you are crying out. I know your heart very well. I will give your family an opportunity. Therefore, observe carefully what I am about to show you."

* The Branches And Leaves From The Tree of Life Move About

Inside the secret room, the leaves from a certain tree were moving as though they were alive. The tree appeared very healthy, refreshed, and vividly green. It was very noticeable how this particular tree looked so refreshed. I had no idea that the tree I was looking at was the Tree of Life. The branches began to wriggle toward me. The branches looked similar as a sedum or ivy stem. Once the branches reached me, they began to touch my head and body. I became tickled to the point of annoyance. Father God, Jesus, and Moses watched how I reacted. I had been crying and distressed about my family and brothers" salvation and now I was being tickled by a tree. I said, "What kind of three is this? Why is it bothering me? Why is it touching me and aggravating me?" As I spoke and was irritated, I grabbed one of the branches, tore it and threw it onto the floor.

Father God was very surprised at my unexpected behavior and said, "Oh, Pastor Kim! Why did you do that? Why! I esteem this tree and its branches. I think highly and honorably of this tree. Why did you do such a thing?" Within that moment, I thought to myself, 'Ahhh! This must be the Tree of Life which Father God so honorably thinks and cares about.' I was in shock and ashamed. I began to step back. Then it happened in a second.

How on earth does a tree move like that to irritate me? I instantly regretted my actions. I should have asked Father God first about the tree. I have made a public display of my impatience and bad temper in the heavenly sanctuary. Jesus murmured in disappointment. This incident was due to my ignorance. I quickly fell on my knees and dropped my head down and continuously asked for forgiveness. Father God then whipped away my nervousness. He began to explain, "Pastor Kim, listen carefully! Due to your carelessness, several of the leaves have fallen from the Tree of Life. All trees and plants in this room are very dear to Me. However, among all the plant life, I especially esteem the leaves from the Tree of Life. I preciously take care of them. The leaves from the Tree of Life represent the souls of men. In fact, they are directly connected to the souls of men. The leaves on the floor that you have made fall represent the souls of men. Look!" As Father God meticulously explained, I was very sorry for my action. I was amazed at His kindness.

Despite the branch losing many leaves, the tree continuously moved toward me and it appeared as though it was trying to express something to me. It attempted to express something by touching my head, face, and my other body parts. What did this mean? What did the actions of the tree represent? I was truly perplexed and curious.

* Is My Family Members' Faith Genuine?

With enormous love, Father God touched me and said, "Very well, now let us distinguish your brothers's faith, whether it is genuine or not. You have importunately asked and you will be shown their faith." I was very apprehensive with the answer I was about to be shown. My heart was racing, but I was still very curious. The leaves that had fallen to the floor began to slowly move and transform. The leaves transformed into my brothers, nephews, and nieces. As I witnessed the scene, I became shocked and instantly screamed. Of all the leaves, only three remained and the rest began to disappear one by one. "Ah! Brothers! My little brother! How can this be?" I felt hopeless and once again the anger began to rage. I immediately plummeted onto the marble floor and began crying hysterically. And again, I rolled and tumbled all about the floor.

"God! Jesus! Trinity God! How can you do this to me? It would have been better if you had not shown this to me! For what reason have you brought me here to give me this anguish? If I had not seen this, I still could have believed that they had been saved. What are you doing to me?" I was not able to control my sadness and I cried unceasingly. Not knowing how long I was wailing, I eventually fainted.

Whenever, I had encouraged my brothers or other people about their faith, I had always advised or encouraged them in a nonchalant manner. I would say as such: "Be faithful." I did not go beyond that statement because I was more concerned about their feelings. I did not want to step on their toes, in other words, their pride. However, after I had been shown the true nature of their current faith, I was totally lost. I did not know what to do. I was totally perplexed.

Father God was gently patting my back while I was unconscious. When I recovered, He said, "Pastor Kim, stop crying now. You well know that this is a place where there are no tears or sorrow. Do you not know?" But once again, I continued to plead for my brothers" salvation. He said, "Very well, very well. Stop your panting and observe the hidden sins of your brothers. Look carefully." Father God showed me the clear picture. Moreover, He said, "Your brothers have repented. In fact, they know they have repented, yet, they have no fruits of repentance. They have repented with no evidence. There is no broken heart, no sincerity!" Anguished, I earnestly asked, "Father, but still, please have pity on them. Please have compassion toward them."

"For thus saith the Lord, Thy bruise is incurable, and thy wound is grievous. There is none to plead thy cause that thou mayest be bound up: thou hast no healing." (Jeremiah 30:12-13)

"The heart is deceitful above all things, and desperately wicked; who can know it? I the Lord search the heart, I try the reins, even to give every man according to his ways, and according to the fruit of his doings." (Jeremiah 17:9-10)

I did not know how much I had pleaded. I felt as though I had pleaded forever. I tumbled and rolled on the floor covered in tears. My face and nose were covered with mucus. Father God then finally promised that He would watch and be with me. "Very well, I understand your heart! I know you care very much for your brothers. I will answer your prayers. But I despise their religious ways and their religious faith. I hate it the most." Father God promised that He would save my brothers and their family members. However, there was one condition. They had to accept the opportunity in faith. I thanked Father God with an audible voice and then worshipped Him as I cried.

As some time passed, I closely paid attention to the transparent wall from across the room. Inside the transparent wall, the Holy Fire vigorously blazed up. I could feel the intense heat from where I was standing. It was very hot; my body felt the burning sensation. As I starred at it, Father God spoke. "Pastor Kim! You will soon be entering that room. Therefore, prepare yourself with sufficient prayers. You have to seriously prepare yourself, physically and spiritually. Do you understand?" Without hesitation, I answered loudly: "Amen!"

Since Father God personally spoke to me, I resolved with my

pledge. 'I must pass through the room to the end.' I then asked God. "Are there any other fire tunnels or Holy blazing rooms in heaven?" Father replied, "Yes, there are many other rooms as such! Pastor Kim, you will enter a Holy Fire blazing room and then another Holy Fire blazing room, and so forth. The first room you will enter will be less intense and then it will become more intense as you go through each room. I will pour all my powers unto you. You must not become arrogant or prideful. Countless of my servants have become very arrogant due to the power I have given them. As a result, many of them have ended up in hell. I am very distressed! Pastor Kim, you will have to humble yourself more than ever. As miracles and power manifest and increase dramatically, the people will exalt you. Therefore, you must be more cautious than ever. Be very careful with the spiritual powers you obtain.

I have no idea why God has granted this enormous task and grace to the servant who is weak and incompetent. I didn't think I was going to handle the responsibility. Before anything happened, I was already worrying. I must not become arrogant or prideful. As thoughts of worry filled my mind, Father God spoke to me as He caressed my back. "Pastor Kim! In commemoration of your visit to the secret room, you will now visit hell to observe what needs to be observed!"

I was shocked at Father God's command. "Father God! I cannot visit hell. I cannot handle it. My physical appearance is a not what it appears. I am a very timid man. I am scared to go. In fact, I do not want to go!" Laughing out loud, Father God said, "It is all right! Your current faith is more than enough to handle the situation." But I persistently resisted and said with a loud tone. "God! No way! I am very frightened." As Jesus laid His hands on me and prayed, He said, "I will grant you all powers." Even with His encouraging words, I still resisted to the very end. As a result, I did not have to visit hell.

Father God and Jesus said, "Pastor Kim! Now do you believe all that we have shown you? Henceforth, you will no longer refrain from documenting all the things that I show you, the things I have and will show you of heaven, hell, and the identities of the devil. You must fulfill your task; many souls are at stake. They must properly and correctly believe in Me. If you do as I command, an unimaginable blessing will be granted upon you. Obey to the end!"

Father God and Jesus took turns as they caressed me. For some reason, I have been granted special grace. I only consider myself as a sinner and a foolish servant. Father God's majesty is unimaginable. It is too difficult to describe with physical eyes or with a finite mind. In some special way, Father God has encountered with a sinner like me. How will I ever express in human words my experience with mighty God? It is impossible to describe, write, or define God in human terms of what I need to express about Him.

God told me to keep this room a secret and not divulge it to anyone. I had found out at a later time that this secret room was a heavenly sanctuary. I was very ignorant about this place. It was after a few months later that the Lord had meticulously explained to me of its importance. He then commanded me to disclose the information to the public. It was titled, "The Secret Room." I began to write the third book which was about the secret room.

I came out of the sanctuary and stood in front of God's throne for a long time. As I stood in front of God"s throne, I looked and viewed over space and galaxy. As Father God sat on His throne, there were no places where He could not reach: either heaven, the galaxy, space or earth. It appeared as though all of creation in the universe was under Father God's feet.

"But now thus saith the Lord that created thee, O Jacob, and He that formed thee, O Israel, Fear not: for I have redeemed thee, I have called thee by thy name; thou art mine. When thou passet through the waters, I will be with thee: and through the rivers, they shall not overflow thee: when thou walkest through the fire, thou shall not be burned: neither shall the flame kindle upon thee. For I am the Lord thy God, the Holy One of Israel, thy Saviour: I gave Egypt for thy ransom, Ethiopia and Seba for thee." (Isaiah 43: 1-3)

Father God has appointed and called someone like me. I consider myself a very doubtful person on every matter. I am very grateful that He has called me, but at the same rate, I am very nervous. Since I have now witnessed and experienced the situation of my relatives's salvation, I can no longer question it. In spite of my sinful, rude, and complaining attitude, He had kindly showed and explained it on terms I could understand. God's ways are higher. Due to my finite level of understanding, He had to illustrate it in a way in which I was able to realize it. I will never forget the encounter I had with Trinity God in the heavenly sanctuary. Always engraved in my memory will be the excitement and impressions I experienced.

* Mrs. Kang, Hyun-Ja - Annoying The Lord

Mrs. Kang, Hyun-Ja: Sister Baek, Bong-Nyu was once again admitted to the hospital for her back pain. Jesus accompanied me to visit Sister Baek. The Lord walked in front of me as we entered the hospital. As we arrived, we sat on her bed and began speaking with her. I asked the Lord with insistence. "Lord! The Pastor's home is located in one of the best dwelling places in heaven. Why is mine so far away from his home? Lord! Can you move my house to the nice neighborhood in heaven?" Jesus answered, "You must earn the rewards to have your home be located there." Sister Baek, Bong-Nyu laughed and said, "Mrs. Kang, Hyun-Ja, you have a such a tall home. What more do you want?" The Lord slanted his brows and said, "Saint Bong-Nyu, do not even start with my bride

Kang, Hyun-Ja! After I had granted her with the gift of prophecy and spiritually opened eyes, she has persistently asked me questions and favors all day long. I do not know what to do with her!" We then all laughed for quite some time. Sister Baek, Bong-Nyu asked me what I was so curious about to ask Jesus questions all day long. The Lord then said, "That is what I am saying!"

I then asked another question: "My beloved Jesus! Last time you had said that the heavenly saints can come down to earth. Is this true? That is possible? Is there any scripture to back that up? I know that heavenly angels can come down to earth to protect the saints. If I remember correctly, there are scripture to justify that in the Bible. The souls who have already passed on can come back to earth? Is this possible?"

Jesus said, "What is impossible for me? However, the souls that have gone to hell can no longer come back to earth. Once someone goes to hell, it is final. If I grant permission, the souls in heaven can come down to earth to visit. Father God supervises the visit."

Sister Baek, Bong-Nyu and I asked, "Lord! Can you bring Biblical men from heaven now?" The Lord said, "Not yet! I esteem the saints from the Lord's Church. These days, I talk about them all the time. The saints from the Lord's church zealously pray and worship God in a very special way. The heavenly souls desire to see and meet the saints from the Lord's Church. They ask me if I can take them with me whenever I come to visit the church. In heaven, the souls are only able to watch the Lord's church through a screen which angels record with video cameras. Your worship and service delights God that very much. The Lord's Church is the top of the news."

I asked the Lord. "Jesus! Do you publicize about us?" The Lord answered, "Of course, I publicize it personally. This is why all the souls in heaven know about you. They are very intrigued by it."

I once again mentioned the subject of moving my home to the best neighborhood in heaven. As I asked, the Lord replied. "From this night forward, you will have to please me. Start making your confession of the love you have for me and please me. Can you do that?" With lovely body gestures, I answered "Yes" to Him in a soft, charming voice. Jesus said, "Saint Kang, Hyun-Ja, all you know is Me! If you only love Me, what about Pastor Kim? The Lord then laughed. The Lord moved my home to the best neighborhood in heaven.

Perhaps, it was due to my faith and persistent pleas. With only one command, the Lord had moved my home. Therefore, I decided to put in more requests. I asked for the homes of our other church members to be moved to the best neighborhood in heaven as well. However, the Lord required them to earn the reward and to continue praying.

* The Evil Spirits Are Provoked

Sister Baek Bong Nyu: My back was in extreme pain and I decided to check myself into the hospital. With physical therapy once a day, the pain was eventually manageable. Pastor and Mrs. Kang, Hyun-Ja had visited me while I was in the hospital. With my spiritual eyes, I was able to see the Lord Jesus and the Holy Spirit accompany them. As soon as the Lord appeared, all the evil spirits in the room became startled and began fleeing in all directions. Within a few moments, all of the evil spirits had departed from the room. The Pastor and his wife comforted me as we performed service. The Lord considered the pastor's wife his fiancé and He especially treated her well. I was very envious with the special treatment she received from the Lord. Mrs. Kang, Hyun-Ja always expressed her love toward Jesus. The Lord loved her for her expressiveness. She didn't even care if people in the hospital saw how she acted for Jesus. She would show her love for Jesus at anytime.

As the Pastor worshipped and sang, he looked around to see if others were watching. He then began to dance in a humorous way. His wife began to follow suit as she danced, but she was dancing in the Holy Spirit. Jesus imitated the pastor. When Jesus laughs, He is very loud. Whenever Jesus loudly laughs, I would think to myself: 'The Lord is Spirit. How can Spirit who is the Lord laugh so much like a human?' I had realized that Father God, Jesus, and the Holy Spirit also possess attributes just like us. Trinity God can either express joy or sadness.

* The Lord Said That We Are Created In His Image

The joyful period only lasted for a short time. Once the pastor and his wife departed, the evil spirits suddenly returned. There were seven other beds in my room. An elderly sick women occupied each of those beds. An evil spirit would stand and occupy a bed at each headboard. The evil spirits giggled as they glanced around with their evil stares. "Hey! You may be going to heaven but these people are going to hell with me. I hope I have provoked you! Evangelize as best you can; it will be very difficult. Hehehehe!" The evil spirits looked just like the ones I had seen on television that were on horror series. These were the evil spirits that escorted the souls of the condemned. It was very creepy. My body was covered with goose bumps.

Since I was in the hospital, I was not allowed to shout or speak out in an audible tone. Instead, I prayed in tongues. Whenever I saw an unbeliever, I could see their bodies filled with evil spirits. Among the group of evil spirits, the ones that escort condemned souls to hell are responsible for unbelief. They are the ones that cause spiritual blindness for the gospel. They also set up unbelieving people to die in accidents in order to drag them to hell. Other believers who have spiritual eyes such as myself can clearly witness these events.

March 25th, 2005 (Friday)

Sermon scripture: "And as they led him away, they laid hold upon one Simon, a Cyrenian, coming out of the country, and on him they laid the cross, that he might bear it after Jesus." (Luke 23:26)

Kim Joseph: Tonight, we commemorate the suffering of our Lord, Jesus. Jesus took up the cross and walked up to Golgotha. He died on the cross and had poured out His blood for us. Remembering Jesus at the cross, the congregation of the church members and I listened to the preaching of the Word.

* Jesus's Suffering Scene And Reenactment

The Pastor preached about Simon, the Cyrenian who was visiting from the countryside and how he had watched and then took up the Lord"s cross. During the middle of the sermon, as the Pastor fervently spoke, I saw a vision. I saw a multitude of people and I heard the babbling of voices and it was loud. I saw Jesus standing in the center of the crowd and He was wearing the crown of thorns. The Lord was profusely bleeding from all of His body.

The vivid scene was clearly shown in front of my eyes as though I was viewing a movie. I noticed that I was standing in the middle of the crowd. The Lord was looking at me and our eyes met. Several days ago as the week to commemorate the Lord"s suffering began, I concentrated on praying. I prayed to be like Simon and to take up the cross. I prayed to experience the carrying of the heavy cross and to experience the pain of it.

Jesus, being in front of me, had been beaten up so much that His wounds were deep and at every part of His body. He bled unceasingly and profusely. The blood dripped down to the ground and formed small puddles. I ran hysterically around the crowd shouting, "Why are you doing this? Please do not hit my Jesus. Please stop doing this." I continued shouting to persuade the people from harassing and beating on Jesus. But they did not care; they continued to beat on the Lord and found pleasure from doing it.

The worst was when the people spit as they ridiculed Jesus. They spit nasty, sticky phlegm at the Lord. The Lord's face and hair were smeared with spit and phlegm. As I came close to Jesus, I tried to support Him as He was on the ground. The Lord grabbed me with His hand that was soaked by blood. He looked at me and said, "Oh, it is you, Joseph! I am in suffering. The people are mocking and assaulting me. It is all for you! Follow Me and keep your eyes only on Me."

As the Lord stood up, taking up the cross, He said, "The saints in the Lord's Church, follow Me, now follow Me!" As Jesus commanded, the Pastor stopped preaching and stepped down from the altar. We all lined up in a single row. As Jesus took up His cross to His back, He walked in front of the line and declared, "Lord's Church, my flock! Focus on Me, keep your eyes on Me as you follow Me. When you see me fall as I walk taking up the cross, you must completely repent on the spot where I fell! I am recreating the scene, especially for you." Once He had proclaimed His statement, He began to walk first in line, taking up His cross on His back.

The Lord was now walking between the chairs of the church and around the inside of the church. With my spiritual eyes, I could clearly see the scene vividly. The scenes continued, one after another. I followed behind Jesus as the Pastor was behind me. Mrs. Kang, Hyun-Ja, Sister Baek, Bong-Nyu, Deaconess Shin were following behind, respectively. We continued to follow Jesus in this order. We were all covered with tears. As Jesus carried the cross, He fell many times as He was weakened from the weight of the cross and the beatings. The church members who had their spiritual eyes opened witnessed the whole event of the Lord suffering as we followed Him.

* Falling 14 Times

With the cross on His back, the Lord walked and fell. We also instantly fell to our knees and repented in tears on the very spot where Jesus fell. We remorsefully repented for a long time. The Lord endured with much difficulty as He got up. Once again, the Lord took up the cross, laying it on His back, and began taking His steps. The Lord staggered and swayed as he continued to walk. He took one step at a time. Walking behind the Lord and closely observing the scene, I was not able to bear the pain in my heart. As I looked up into the sky and down to the ground, I cried profusely.

I remorsefully repented. Moreover, all the members of the church congregation remorsefully repented as well.

The Lord continuously fell and got back up throughout His walk up Golgotha. The Lord was only able to take a few steps before He fell again. Whenever the Lord would fall, the Roman soldier was there to whip Jesus without mercy. The Lord groaned in pain as blood splattered from His body. The blood stains on the ground were clearly visible. The voices from the evil people were chaotic and pandemonium. The noise annoyed my ears. The people appeared as though they were enjoying the suffering of Jesus. With the physical eyes, one would just see the church members walking in circles inside the church. But with the spiritual eyes, we were witnessing the Lord getting whipped and tormented during His walk.

My temper exploded; I could no longer watch in silence. "Hey! You evil people! Don't do that! Why are you tormenting the Lord? Why?" My pleading faded away from the noise of the crowd. The Lord continued to fall and get up. As we watched Him, the Lord fell a total of fourteen times. At each spot where Jesus fell, we fervently repented in tears. Time had elapsed quickly — 3 to 4 hours had already passed.

Jesus groaned more severely. This time the Lord appeared as though He was not going to get up. I loudly shouted, "Pastor, Sisters and Brothers! Jesus has fallen and He looks like He will not get up. What should I do?"

* Joseph Takes Up The Cross Of Jesus

Compassion filled my heart as I saw the Lord fall to the ground. I wanted to help the Lord. And as I tried to help Him, a Roman soldier using his index finger gestured for me to come. "Hey! You! Come here!" When the Roman soldier shouted, I suddenly became frightened. I was in shock. I thought my heart was going to stop. I thought to myself, this is only a vision. This was not a real situation. I hesitated and decided not to answer the command of the Roman soldier. Then the Roman soldier drew his sword and rushed toward me. I resisted, struggled, and kicked. "Ah! What are you doing?" The Roman soldier placed the sword at my neck and threatened me. "You take up the cross this instance. Now! If you don't, I will cut you up! Take up this cross now!"

I thought to myself, 'How can this be happening?' I was very confused and afraid. I began to meticulously explain what was happening to my father, the Pastor. The Pastor told me to obey Jesus's command.

Tonight's sermon was about Simon from Cyrene who had carried the cross for Jesus. Like Simon, I had to carry the cross and follow Jesus. I was in danger of having my head cut off if I made a mistake. I prayed for the opportunity as Simon had carried the cross for the Lord. I had never expected this to come true, not even in my dreams.

I did not expect my prayer to be answered this quickly. I was astonished and shocked and did not know how to react. As the scene unfolded in front of my sight, I did not initially dare to carry the cross. But now the situation was unavoidable; I had to carry the cross for Jesus. The weight of the cross was unimaginable. It was very heavy. I began to see Golgotha from a distance. It was still some distance away.

As I carried the cross, my right shoulder began to swell. I was in pain. I did not know what to do. Up to this point, I had not realized how heavy the cross weighed. Carrying it required so much strength and exertion. Realizing this fact, I cried and repented. Bearing the weight of the cross was very painful.

That same night, after our prayer rally, I checked my right shoulder once I arrived home. My right shoulder was swollen and red. I became ill and my body severely ached. I almost missed school due to my sickness. In the morning, my mother applied a muscle relief ointment onto my shoulder to help with the swelling. However, the pain was still intense and did not go away. My swelling and pain continued for several days.

While I was praying, Jesus came and said, "My beloved Joseph! I had taken the cross and carried it. It was very difficult. Wasn't it? For all of you, I had poured my blood and water to die on the cross. Therefore, Joseph, when you face difficult or hard situations, always remember Me. Do not forget! If you remember, no matter how difficult the situation may be, you will endure. Do you understand?"

"Yes, Lord! Thank you. It was my honor to carry the cross. Thank you so much for giving me the opportunity to carry it." As the Lord softly touched my swollen shoulder, He said, "In the future, you will be my servant and I will use you greatly throughout the world. You will receive great power. Therefore, humble yourself and be quick to obey, even to the end."

* The Least Of The Villages In Heaven

Kim, Joo-Eun: My mother asked me to go find out what place in heaven does my mother's paternal grandmother and her maternal grandmother live. I was going to check by asking the Lord. My mother's paternal grandmother and maternal grandmother accepted the Lord as their Savior and King right before they had passed. Therefore, they were in heaven. They had not done much for the Lord, therefore they were living on the outer edges of heaven now. The place where they were residing in heaven had homes built like subdivisions. They had one level and all looked the same.

Jesus had said that He built the home for paternal grandmother as a single story, level house after He had seen her evangelize to some people at the park for a few days. This had happened right before her passing. I had visited heaven and went to where grandmother resided to check it out for myself.

In heaven, receiving the love of the Lord is the best joy any saint can experience. It is the best happiness. In heaven, the grandmothers were not receiving the complete fullness of God, but they were honored and very happy just being in heaven. Part of our reward is to receive the fullness of the Lord's love. The grandmothers were very close to going to hell and their last days made the difference. In heaven, they looked very youthful and they were transformed beautifully. They looked great!

Currently, the talk of heaven was about the Lord's Church. The talk was resonant everywhere. As I arrived in heaven to meet my mothers's grandmothers, the neighbors who were close to my grandmother's homes rushed as a group and marvelously observed me.

I felt like some kind of superstar. I was thrilled and happy. I did not know what to do. "Saint grandmothers! Are you able to recognize who I am?" They replied, "Of course, we know you. There are no heavenly saints who do not know the saints of the Lord's Church. Our beloved Jesus speaks about the Lord's Church daily. We hear the news about you every day. Jesus is very pleased. The service in the Lord's church is extraordinary and the Lord boasts around heaven how the service at your church is run delightfully and joyfully. But please stop calling us grandmother. Call us Saints. It is an honor that you visit us." They were very humble.

I asked, "You know my mother, right? Saint Kang, Hyun-Ja? She had asked me that when I visit heaven to check and meet you. Saints, it has been two years since you had passed.

Does Jesus often visit you?" They replied, "We usually see Jesus from a distance. In fact, Jesus has never visited us here in person." I asked why. They said that it is due to the fact that they had never really done the Lord''s work on earth. In fact, they had barely made it to heaven. It was due to the fact they had accepted the Lord as Savior and King right before they had passed. Therefore, they did not receive any special attention and love from the Lord. They said that they were average citizens of heaven.

They said, "As you continue the Lord's work, do as much as you can. Your home and reward will be large based on your work for Him. Saint Joo-Eun! Do the Lord's work as much as you can. One receives much love from Jesus if one have a taller home. The taller the home, the more love they receive. You and the Lord's Church saints must be very happy, blessed." As they spoke, they feebly spoke. And yet, they said that heaven is a great place and they love it very much. Whenever I had asked or wanted to discuss the things that had happened to them on earth, they waved their hands and said that they did not want to discuss or think about it. I was just curious.

I said, "Granny Saints! If so, would you like me to request any special favors from Jesus, especially about Him visiting you often?" When I had asked that, they jumped up and down and danced in joy. "What? Really? Ah! That would be a fine thing! We would not desire of anything more." I asked Jesus: "My beloved Jesus! Could you visit the homes of my maternal and paternal grandmothers?" The Lord was silent. When I repeated and pleaded the request continuously, He answered and said He would do that. Both my grandmothers were in so much joy. They were very thrilled. They respectfully bowed to Jesus.

I said to Jesus. "Lord, I will later ask my grandmothers if you had visited them at their places or not." The Lord laughed and said, "All right, you have the same persistence as your mother." So I replied, "That's right Lord! My mother educated me like that and she gave me a secret mission in which is to ask you a special favor." The Lord and I laughed out loud.

Other souls from my grandmothers's neighborhood came and witnessed the Lord visit my grandmothers. They were envious of the visit. Joyously, I said to my grandmothers, "Saints! I will ask of the Lord to visit you more often." Both grandmothers jumped for joy when they heard my words.

April 10th, 2005 (Sunday Evening)

"All things are delivered unto me of my Father: and no man knoweth the Son, but the Father; neither knoweth any man the Father, save the Son, and he to whomsoever the Son will reveal him." (Matthew 11:27)

* Swimming In The Crystal Clear Ocean

Kim, Joo-Eun: Calling by my nickname, my beloved Jesus called and asked me. "Freckles, would you like to go to heaven?" I instantly replied, "Yes, Jesus." As I held the Lord's hand, we arrived at the gate of Heaven. The angels that guarded the entrance opened wide the gates of Heaven as they saw us coming toward them. The Lord took me to the crystal clear ocean. I was now witnessing what I had only heard from other people. I now had the opportunity to view the crystal clear ocean in person. The ocean shone like a jewel. I noticed Sister Yoo-Kyung who had arrived earlier, splashing and swimming in the ocean. She was having so much fun with Yeh Jee. Yeh Jee was the daughter of deaconess Shin. I loved the water but I did not really know how to swim.

At first, I was a bit afraid of entering the crystal clear ocean. It was very novel to me. The Lord noticed and said, "Freckles! Do not be afraid. Look at Yeh Jee and Yoo-Kyung. They are swimming well, are they not? Stop worrying. Would you like to swim with me? Hurry." Jesus held my hand and He led me to the ocean as I resisted. But as the Lord held my hand, my fear began to somewhat go away. But I was still a bit afraid.

I gained more confidence as the Lord began teaching me how to swim. As I slowly learned, I was feeling great. I thrust my left arm and then my right arm to swim forward. The Lord held on to both my hands. As I tightly grabbed His hand, I paddled with both my feet. I played and water was splashing as I paddled rigorously. The

Lord complimented me. "All right! You are doing great! Good job!" While I swam with the Lord, Yoo-Kyung and Yeh Jee glanced at what I was doing. They were laughing in amusement for awhile. As they swam, Yoo-Kyung shouted, "Joo-Eun! You are a little late. But that is all right! Do not be afraid. Keep it up!" Yeh Jee shouted, "Sister Joo-Eun! It is me, Yeh Jee!"

Yeh Jee looked very beautiful as she swam. She would always wear a shining hair band around her head. When she was on earth, she was terribly sick. Her stomach was full of water and her face was always pale white. She had lost all her hair from the chemotherapy. She was always sad. However, Yeh Jee's appearance in heaven was very beautiful, more beautiful than any of the princesses in all the story books.

The crystal clear ocean was so clean that it was emulating light itself. It was absolutely amazing. I noticed a unique thing: at the bottom of the ocean lay a floor of hexagon shaped lines. Each hexagon form enclosed the face of a member at the Lord's Church. The faces were carved inside the hexagons. During our fun times, when we expressed our funniest facial expressions, that expression was captured and carved into the hexagon. It looked very real, like a real picture. I was very surprised at the scene. I asked the Lord.

"Jesus, why are the faces of the members from the Lord's Church engraved at the bottom of the ocean?" The Lord answered: "I carved them in. The members of the Lord's church make me very happy. I made them since I felt so delighted. How do you feel about it? Does it make you happy to see it? I replied loudly, "Yes, Lord!"

I was busy swimming with the Lord. I had never experienced this kind of event throughout my life. Sister Yoo-Kyung visits heaven every single day and when she returns, she would always brag about swimming in the crystal clear ocean. She would boast loudly for a long time; I would be so envious of her trip. Now, my wish

had come true. I now understand what she was describing to us on earth. It is a feeling of blessedness in the highest to play in the ocean. In fact, I was able to talk with all kinds of different fishes. I will never forget this time,
especially talking to fish.

* Alcohol And cigarettes

Kim, Joseph: Since my eyes are opened spiritually, I am most often very surprised with the spiritual state of other people. At any time, I am able to see their spiritual state. I am able to see when I walk by them or whenever I speak with them. It does not matter if my physical eyes are closed or opened. The Lord shows me the spiritual aspects of other people.

The Lord also taught me when to speak and when not to speak. He had strictly distinguished the difference to me. Whenever I was unaware and spoke freely, the Lord rebuked me. I had to have the Lord's permission on every little matter. It was very difficult and tiring. However, when it came to hanging out with kids my age, the Lord never told me not to hang out with them.

The Lord had told me that I could hang out with them and have fun but to be very careful of their deceiving spirits. Around noontime, on the way to church, I happened to pass by the outside bar that was open. The people were drinking hard liquor and beer. They were having a good time partying. I felt like vomiting from the unpleasant smell of liquor and cigarette smoke. I passed by holding my breath. However, I decided to go back to the outside bar and closely observe the drunk people. I wanted to know with my spiritual eyes what could be in the glasses of liquor and observe the circumstances.

The drunk people held onto big beer glasses. I was very surprised as I saw the beer glasses with my spiritual eyes. I was not sure of what I was seeing, so I double-checked by opening my eyes more widely. In the glasses of beer, I could see wriggling snakes. They looked like king cobras. The small glasses of hard liquor were filled with small stringy snakes. The scene was very disgusting. I could not watch anymore.

The people did not care about anything except drinking more. In fact, they appeared to be competing with each other on who could drink more or faster. As they drank in a binge, the small stringy snakes that looked like king cobras said, "Oh, I feel great!" The snakes shook their tails and went down the throats of the drinkers. Jesus appeared next to me and said, "Joseph! Watch this scene very carefully and remember. Then go tell Pastor Kim to write this scene in the book." The people cheered and shouted as they toasted and drank.

Moreover, in this scene, as some people took out their cigarettes and lit them, they inhaled and blew out the smoke. When they blew out the smoke, a dark smoke continuously blew out from their noses and mouths. Suddenly, in an instant, the smoke transformed into a king cobra snake. They snakes came out from the smokers" noses and mouths but they went back in as the smokers inhaled.

Bizarrely, when the snakes re-entered the smokers's bodies, the appearance of the snakes became more heinous than when they initially came out from the smokers's noses and mouths. As the snakes re-entered the smokers's bodies, the snakes had an evil facial expression. As the partying continued, the number of smokers increased. The liquor glasses were all filled with different, small stringy snakes and the snakes from the cigarettes. The people were really drinking and smoking snakes. The party was really a party of snakes. As the party drew to a close, I realized it was not a party of people drinking and smoking, but it was a party of snakes eating people. The scene was revolting and I was getting sick witnessing the event. I decided to leave.

Whenever I see drunk people walking unsteadily, I am able to see the various kinds of large and small snakes coiled around the drunks from the top of their heads down to their toes. Both of the drunk person's eyes are covered with a snake sitting coiled up and hissing. There was also a snake sitting coiled up on the drunk person's head and it glanced at me evilly as it hissed at me with its tongue.

As people smoke cigarettes and they pass by me, the smoke lingers in the air and with our physical eyes, we see it fade and dissipate into the air. But in reality, the smoke turns into snakes which comes from the smokers's mouth and then instantly go back into their bodies. When the snakes enter the bodies of smokers, they do not come out from the bodies of smokers on their own. Moreover, the snakes lay their eggs inside the bodies of smokers and as a result, more snakes dwell inside their bodies. Within time, swarms of snakes are housed within the smokers's bodies.

I thought I would only witness these events or the demon snakes from outside the church. However, some Christians from throughout South Korea who would visit our church to pray and be blessed would end up screaming. They screamed and fell on the floor as they hissed with their tongues as the Pastor would draw close to pray for them. I witnessed countless scenes of such events and still continue to do so presently.

When drunks and smokers speak, I could hear them speak though they were speaking with a crooked tongue. The sounds of their words were crooked. As I see and hear them speak with my spiritual eyes, I could see that the snakes were hissing and speaking in their place. As I witness these accounts, I am startled all the time. When the drunks vomit to the ground, I am able to see coiled snakes on the vomit. In the market stores, where they sell all types of liquor, I can see swarms of stringy snakes swimming and dancing in the bottles. I am always able to see that.

* Evil Spirits Constantly Attack Pastor Kim

Pastor Kim, Yong-Doo: It has been a long times since I began my restless endeavor to publish this book exposing the devils's identities. I just do not know why my progress is so slow. However, I know that Jesus and the Holy Spirit are always protecting me. Despite their protection, the forces of the devil continuously seek an opportunity to attack without ceasing. At any given moment of weakness and absent mindedness, I am attacked without mercy. The forces of the devil will stab at me with sharp objects.

Without the Holy Spirit inside of me, I would not have been able to complete the books. Moreover, it would have been too difficult to write without His assistance. At times, the Lord would allow the evil spirits to attack me as a test to improve and encourage my faith. Nevertheless, the correct amount of pressure and testing has resulted in many spiritual benefits.

For example, one day, I was praying and writing at the same time. I was in deep concentration when I was stabbed on the back of my right hand with a sharp object by an evil spirit. The evil spirit had stabbed me as it passed by. It happened so fast that I did not even have a chance to react. For several hours, I was in pain and the pain was unbearable. Moreover, blood began to ooze from the stabbed area. I know people who have not experienced or seen such spiritual attacks will have a difficult time believing in this event.

I asked the Lord, "Lord! Why are these types of attacks inflicted on me when you are protecting me?" The Lord was silent for some time. After a long silence, the Lord then answered me. "Such attacks are for the benefit of the Kingdom and you will be rewarded. You will not be able to write about the various attacks by the evil spirits without first having to experience them." The Lord then touched the area of my pain. Whenever I was in the process of writing the book, the Lord would vividly show Himself to me. He would also vividly speak to me. He would do so on special occasions as well. During other times, He did not do so. The Lord had also told me that I had sinned by exposing some confidential information some time ago. Therefore, I still had many things to learn and realize. Even now, with my physical eyes, I am able to see some activities of the evil spirits. Whenever the evil spirits attack me, they use guerrilla tactics. They would pass closely by me, and as they passed, they would throw a spear, piercing my body. If they were at a distance, they would continuously throw stones. I would always be in severe pain and torment from the lethal attacks by the evil spirits. In some severe instances, I had screamed and fell on to the floor as the unbearable pain gripped my body.

Chapter 5
Visiting Heaven In
A Group With The Lord

April 15th, 2005 (Friday)

Sermon scripture: "Ye therefore, beloved, seeing ye know these things before, beware lest ye also, being led away with the error of the wicked, fall from your own steadfastness. But grow in grace, and in the knowledge of our Lord and Saviour Jesus Christ. To him be glory both now and for ever. Amen." (2 Peter 3:17-18)

* Jesus Punished My Father

Kim, Joseph: When I returned home after school, I heard mother and father arguing over something that I considered trivial. I carefully listened from the next room. They were arguing over the change of service time. It may not be my place to comment, but fighting over a trivial matter is shameful and I feel sorry for them.

Adults are weird. Generally, my mother and father experience a great relationship, but a bad seed can grow. They water the bad seed with their impatience and soon, they fight as though they will devour each other. I am not able to understand. I wonder if other couples who are in the ministry have the same problem. At first, they comment with a few negative words to one another and then began to disagree. As the conversation continues, their voices began to rise. Although they have spiritual eyes open, I guess fights in the flesh are inevitable. My little sister, Joo-Eun, and I sometimes argue as well.

I instantly ran to my mother and father and shouted, "Please stop! Why are you two acting like little kids! Jesus is watching you argue; He is standing next to you. The Lord feels troubled. If you continue to argue, I'll leave the house this instance!" I was on the verge of exploding in anger. But the Lord winked at me as a signal to be patient. I fell to my knees next to my bed and laid my head against the bed. I closed my eyes as my parents stood next to me watching. Jesus commanded my father and mother to fall on their knees and repent. My parents are always very obedient to the Lord's word. They had no choice but to obey His command. By His facial expression, Jesus was not very pleased. He had brought a long pole which appeared to be reaching the sky. It was very long. He then commanded my father to lie on his face. As soon as my father lay on his face, the Lord used the pole to pound on my father's neck and back. The Lord concentrated on the two specific areas. "Pastor Kim, repent! Pastor Kim, do not be stubborn, change your character! Please do not let your temper explode." I said, "Father! Jesus is smacking you. You need to repent a lot." My father shouted, "Lord! I deserve to be punished: please continuously hit me. Hit me harder!"

Jesus was set in His mind to correct the bad habits of the Pastor. This time, the Lord lashed at my father with a golden colored whip. He stroked him about ten times. However, my father was not in any real pain. After being lashed, the Lord brought a large stick and continued to smack at the back of my father. My father cried and shouted, "Lord! I am very sorry! Please forgive me! I will try to correct my ways but it is difficult. Lord, I deserve to be extremely punished. Please discipline me harder."

I found one thing to be odd. My mother was also on her knees repenting. However, Jesus was admonishing my mother instead of punishing her. The Lord had only severely punished my father. Instantly, I was curious as to what my father's guardian angel was doing. I looked at my father's guardian angel and he was just observing the disciplining of my father. The angel appeared a bit bewildered as he stood a few feet away from the back of Jesus. Father God was grieved at today's incident. He suddenly extended His enormous hand and pointed at the Pastor. In a deep, echoing voice Father God spoke. "Pastor Kim! You have a bad temper." Father God warned my father. Since our family and the church congregation were experiencing special attention from God, our smallest sins were sensitive enough when God reacted.

My father dug his head into the bed and cried. Jesus sat close to my father. It looked like my father's head was between the Lord's knees. As I cried, I pleaded. "Jesus! Jesus! Please forgive my father. Please stop hitting him. Please forgive him. I'll apologize on his behalf." The Lord then stopped punishing my father. He began to pat my father's head and body. The tone of his voice changed; it became soft and comforting. "Pastor Kim, attention! Why do you always have a hot temper?"

On the other side of the room stood several devils in the form of pigs. They stood and watched us. They gloated as they shouted. "Oh! There you go! Why are you trying to restrain your anger? You should let your anger come out more!" Earlier, Father God was also upset. But when Jesus became amicable, Father God became amicable and patted the Pastor's head with His large hand and said, "Do not react in such a way again, never! Go to the church temple and for many hours repent." Jesus placed mother's hand over father's hand and He reconciled them. My father and mother apologized to each other.

"A soft answer turneth away wrath: but grievous words stir up anger." (Proverb 15:1)
"A wrathful man stirreth up strife: but he that is slow to anger appeaseth strife." (Proverb 15:18)

"Be ye angry, and sin not: let not the sun go down upon your wrath. Neither give place to the devil." (Ephesians 4:26-27)

* Tripped By The Body Of A Snake

Kim, Joo- Eun: When I observe my father and mother arguing with my spiritual eyes, I see our church on earth between the two large creatures which were swinging a snake. One creature held the head of the snake while the other held the tail. I saw them swinging the snake with the Lord's Church in the center. The members of the Lord's Church were jumping as the snake was swung between them. Each member jumped; a jump represented a trial and they jumped again and again. My father and mother were jumping at the front of the line. As they jumped, they were tripped by the snake. As soon as my parents fell, the creatures shouted and rejoiced. "Oh! Yes, Pastor Kim finally fell! Our confidence is high. Let us swing faster! Now that the Pastor has fallen, the congregation should be a piece of cake. The congregation members will fall one by one." They then began swinging the snake with a greater speed.

But once my father and mother repented, they began jumping faster and with renewed energy. In fact, they had more energy and were faster than before. If we only repent of our sins, the Lord will always restore us. Moreover, He will grant us greater power. After my vision, the Lord and my family gathered together and sat in the master bedroom. Jesus tapped on my mother's lip and said, "My dear fiancé, Kang, Hyun-Ja! Your mouth is a problem as well." The Lord then tapped at her lips several more times. "Since you have your spiritual eyes opened, you should be transformed. Your personality not being transformed is a problem. My heart is troubled. I will need to get some fresh air in heaven." He then disappeared.

* The Puberty Demon

Mrs. Kang, Hyun Ja: After I reconciled with my husband, my daughter, Joo-Eun began bursting out in a temper. I did not know the reason for it. Perhaps, something happened to her in school. She was very sulky and would not speak. Just moments ago, we felt so blessed, but now I could not understand why we are so easily emotional. "Joseph, take a look at your sister, Joo- Eun! Look what is inside of her…." As soon as I asked Joseph, the Pastor testily spoke out.
"He doesn't have to look inside; it is the devil of puberty inside

her." With a doubt, I said, "Well, that is just impossible! I do not think there is such a thing as a devil of puberty. I really doubt that!"

But Joseph shouted in excitement. "Father! Pastor! How did you know that? You are right! There is a devil of puberty inside of Joo-Eun. That demon is making her sulky and capricious." Joseph was amazed with this revelation.

Once I heard this new revelation, I still could not believe it. We usually know puberty as a normal stage of growing up until adulthood. It is a stage youth go through. It is a stage where the youth become interested in the opposite sex and wonder about finding their love. I just assumed that this was a normal stage in their growth process to adulthood. A devil of puberty? I really cannot understand it.

Joseph stared at Joo-Eun's body with intensity. When he looked inside her, a white dressed devil disguised as a young girl with short hair was the culprit to her capriciousness. In fact, she looked similar to Joo-Eun. This demon caused irritations and made her to complain about everything. Furthermore, the demon caused her to be sulky, disobedient, and made her stare in an evil way. Whatever she did, the demon caused every situation to be a problem and hurdle. With a united heart, we prayed and focused on Joo-Eun. The evil spirit departed and Joo-Eun became herself.

April 16th, 2005 (Saturday Night)

Sermon scripture: "Their heart cried unto the LORD, O wall of the daughter of Zion, let tears run down like a river day and night: give thyself no rest; let not the apple of thine eye cease. Arise, cry out in the night: in the beginning of the watches pour out thine heart like water before the face of the LORD: lift up thy hands toward him for the life of thy young children, that faint for hunger in the top of every street." (Lamentations 2:18-19)

* Visiting Hell As A Group

Pastor Kim, Yong-Doo: We unexpectedly started the prayer rally; it was not planned. All the saints came to church to join in on the rally. "Since all of you desire to have your spiritual eyes opened, I will take all of you to hell as a group today. The people with spiritual eyes will be able to sense and see, but the ones who do not have their spiritual eyes open will only be able to sense. Hell is a very dangerous place, but do not be frightened or nervous. Follow and focus on me." The Lord was at the forefront with Joseph; myself; Mrs. Kang, Hyun-Ja; Joo-Eun; Sister Baek, Bong-Nyu; Lee,Yoo-Kyung; Haak-Sung; Deaconess Shin; and Lee, Kyung-Eun behind the Lord, waiting in a line. We all cautiously followed.

We passed through the galaxy and entered into a dark, spiral-shaped tunnel. As we entered into the dark tunnel, the Lord lined us up and told us to make sure there were no gaps between us. The Lord told us to hold our hands with the person in front of us. He said, "Taking people to hell in a group is not a usual event." He then carefully led us.

After we had passed through the dark tunnel, we could clearly see two separate roads. The right road led to heaven and the left led to hell. We walked toward the road that led to hell. It was cold. There was a strange energy that produced the chill over hell. It was a horrible sensation.

"Entrance of Hell" it stated on the sign. Once we got close to the sign, Jesus told us not
to let go of our hands. He continued to remind us to hold tight and not let go. As the Lord spoke, the church members who had never visited hell were very nervous. Their hearts were uneasy as they walked forward. Sister Baek, Bong-Nyu, Haak-Sung, Yoo-Kyung, and Joo-Eun had already been there and they appeared comfortable with the visit. They handled the situation with confidence.

* Hell Seen By Joseph

Kim, Joseph: The width of the road to hell was unimaginably wide. There were a countless number of people walking toward hell. It looked as if they did not want to go, but some force was making them take the walk down to hell. The enormously wide road began to gradually narrow. In fact, as it became narrow, the road became very difficult to walk on.

The road became so narrow that there was hardly any space to walk on. As a result, most of the people began to fall off the cliff. Many people were falling off the cliff. They screamed as they fell head first. They made every attempt not to fall off. Some grabbed onto other people, whether in front or behind them as they tried to balance themselves. However, they all eventually fell. There were so many falling off from both sides of the narrow road. As I watched the scene, I became very frightened as goose bumps began to cover my body. I could hear the sound of fire from below the narrow road. It sounded like a blow torch with flames that were alive. The flames rose all the way up the sides of the narrow road. The stench of burning flesh was very disgusting. Inside the flames, I could hear the people scream. "Save me!! Hot! Very hot!" Their cries for help echoed clearly in our ears. The flames began to engulf the narrow road and we became afraid. We were unable to continue forward. We heard bombs exploding, but later I witnessed a volcano exploding. The exploding sounds that I had heard were from the volcano. I could see so many naked people jumping up and down inside the burning fire. It is difficult to describe the pain they were in. The black smoke and heat rose and literally transferred onto our bodies. As our view was darkened, we hesitated to move forward. The Lord continuously reminded us to be careful. As He slowly led us forward, He meticulously explained what was going on. And in some cases, He let us experience the places instead of giving us an explanation.

* A Place In Hell With Numerous Worms

As we stepped forward cautiously, one step at a time, someone screamed. "Ahhhhh! What is it?" The people who had their spiritual eyes opened were able to see all things while the ones who did not have their spiritual eyes opened could only sense what was going on. We were passing through an area where countless numbers of worms resided. There were small and large worms all around. They began to coil around our legs as a snake would. They gradually moved up our bodies. There were so many worms. They were in piles as large as mountains. They were always seeking a hole. It didn't matter how small the hole was, they would penetrate any hole. The worms in hell were more loathsome looking than snakes. As we experienced the worms, we all shouted in terror. All of us had made at least one comment or cry. "I am most afraid of worms!! Ahhhhh! Of all the things I hate, I hate worms…" Within that moment, the Pastor loudly said, "Joseph! My rectum suddenly itches. Can you take a look?" I looked and said, "Pastor! There is an enormous worm crawling up your butt hole!" The Pastor replied in terror. "What! What am I going to do?" I said, "I'm not sure. Why don't you try to grab it with your hand and pull it out?" The Pastor replied, "But I cannot see anything!"

The other church members were also battling with the worms as we followed the Lord. After Jesus had observed us for awhile, He said: "Saints of the Lord"s Church! There is the burning Holy Fire within your bodies. So shout "Holy Fire" out loud. When you shout for Holy Fire, the worms will all burn up." All of us shouted, "Holy Fire." As soon as we shouted, all the worms became dust. As we shouted, we sometimes shouted in concert. But we all constantly shouted "Holy Fire" as we walked. The Fire of the Holy Spirit came out of our bodies and burnt all the worms around us. However, the worms did not give up so easily; they unceasingly continued to attack us. I had no idea where all the worms were coming from. I did not understand why they were constantly coming toward us. We were sick and tired of their relentless attacks. After an hour, we had barely escaped from the place of worms.

* A Place In Hell With White Grubs And Maggots

Once again, the Lord led us in a little deeper. We all appeared nervous. I could not tell how far we walked. Joo-Eun was the first to shout. "Ahhhhh!" This place is filled with white grubs and maggots! Oh! Disgusting! Their numbers were so much it was beyond imagination. I realized that the grubs and maggots had heaped up to our waist.

As soon as the grubs and maggots noticed us, they assumed we were their meals. They quickly gathered around us and began to stick on us. We all screamed and hurled. I jumped up and down, stepping on the bugs. Even though we were stepping on them, they did not relent. "There are so many insects." We battled with the insects for a long time, but at the end, we gave up as we become so tired. As we looked at one another, the swarms of maggots began to stick on us up to our heads.

The sensation of grubs and maggots wriggling on our bodies felt horrible. Moreover, they bit us as they crawled up. Their teeth were shaped like a toothed wheel. They were sharp and small. As they attacked, they bit off our flesh. We were scratching our bodies as they painfully stung us. The heat from their bites was unbearable; it made us scratch ourselves even more.

My mother felt repulsed because of the insects. As I looked toward my mother, she was screaming hysterically. "Oh!! Insects are what I hate the most! I hate worms, but I hate maggots the most! What should I do?" It seemed like my mother was most afraid of insects in general. We spent many hours taking the grubs and maggots off our bodies.

* A Place In Hell With Snakes And Centipedes

As we screamed and battled with the maggots, Jesus walked toward another place. We followed behind as He led. Our mind wondered as we were curious to know where He would take us. However, we were frightened. At the edge of the road was nothing but a long drop down. We might have been walking along a cliff. Fierce flames would blaze from the bottom. The flames were so large, we felt we would be swallowed by them. Cautiously looking all around, we continued walking forward. We walked for awhile until I felt something quickly coil around our bodies. It then unmercifully pierced my neck.

This place was filled with snakes and centipedes. Piles of different varieties of snakes and centipedes were everywhere. We were so frightened that we began walking backwards, but the snakes and centipedes approached toward us. The snakes and centipedes coiled onto our arms, legs, and necks. As one snake coiled tightly around the neck of one church member, she began to suffocate. We battled with the snakes and centipedes. They bit and tore into us. We were totally exhausted from the battle. Even though we were out of energy and exhausted, we continued to shout, "Holy Fire" over and over again.

* The Second Highest Ranked Devil Snatches The Pastor Away

As the Lord looked upon us and noticed that we were very tired, He encouraged us. "Get a hold of yourself, my precious flock!" He then led us to another place. As Jesus led us through the other places in hell, the second highest ranked devil appeared and instantly snatched the Pastor away. We were all surprised. "Jesus! Jesus! Something terrible has happened! The king devil has snatched the Pastor away. Hurry, save him! Nothing is impossible for you, Lord!" After we had pleaded to the Lord, He said, "Do not worry. Just let us observe for awhile. Let us see what the devil will do…."

As the devil shouted, "Finally, you have come to hell! Do you know how long I have waited for you? I will take my revenge for the days you had defeated us. Today is the day for my revenge. Pastor Kim, you are a problem!" The devil then took off all his clothes.

The devil brought out a frightening sharp knife and then he began to skin the Pastor. As the church members with spiritually opened eyes saw what was happening, they shouted in terror. "Ahhhh! Jesus! Quickly save the Pastor, please!"

Jesus quietly watched the event. The devil was not aware of our presence. As he jabbed and skinned the flesh from the Pastor's body, the devil spoke to himself, murmuring abusive language. The Pastor shouted, "Hey!! Devil! The Lord is protecting me and I am not able to feel any pain. Your torture is useless and in vain!" I was perplexed and asked the Pastor. "Father! Pastor! You are not in pain?" The Pastor replied, "Joseph, I am tickled. It actually feels good from my head to my toe."

The Pastor continued shouting. "Hey! Devil! You are relieving the areas where I was itching. That is the best you can do? I have Trinity God within me. It does not matter how much you attempt to induce pain; it does not affect me at all. Devil! Hahahahaha! I am not in pain at all. In fact, I feel rather refreshed." The Pastor appeared as though he was actually enjoying this experience.

Sister Baek, Bong-Nyu: The second highest ranked devil was skinning the Pastor alive. The devil even scalped the Pastor. I was only able to see his skull and bones. When I saw the Pastor's appearance, I thought to myself, what a heinous scene. But the scene was also hilarious and I began to laugh uncontrollably. Even though the Pastor was skinned alive and scalped, he was still laughing and making jokes at the devil.

"Jesus! How do I look? Sister Baek, Bong-Nyu! Am I looking handsome?" I asked, "How about you? How do you feel, Pastor?" As a skeleton, the Pastor replied, "My whole body feels very refreshed! I am not in any pain. In fact, I am tickled." The Pastor began laughing out loud.

Jesus laughed and said, "Pastor Kim, you are even able to entertain in hell." After the prayer rally, I said to the Pastor: "Pastor! I did not look down at your private parts." The Pastor replied, "Hey! Do not say that!" Mrs. Kang, Hyun-Ja and the others all laughed hysterically.

* The Sundew Monster

Kim, Joseph: During the middle of Pastor's torment, Jesus pointed out the other side and commanded us to look. It looked like the edge of a cliff. On the cliff stood naked men and women all packed together. There were so many people all crammed together that no space existed between them. They could not even take a step. The people standing along the cliff all began to fall one by one. They were screaming as they fell. In fear, they all held to one another, struggling not to fall. I could no longer watch the scene; I had to turn away.

Jesus explained that those people did not serve God faithfully or properly. They had committed adultery numerous times. At the bottom of the cliff awaited a giant clam that was bigger than a mountain. It was constantly opening and closing its mouth as people fell. As the people fell into the mouth of the clam, it would swallow them. When it opened its mouth, I could see numerous sharp teeth. They were small in nature and compacted all over its mouth. The upper and lower teeth were all synchronized in alignment as the mouth tightly closed. As people fell into the mouth and the teeth closed in on them, the sharp teeth would crush the people's body. They looked as though they were crushed by a meat tenderizer. The sounds of pain from inside the mouth of the clam were more horrific than the screams of people falling. I remember that some time ago I saw a Venus flytrap named "Sundew" on television. The plant hunts for flies and devours them. What I saw on television was similar to what I was witnessing now.

I became consumed with fear as I watched the shocking scene. Jesus said, "My beloved flock from the Lord's Church, how does it feel witnessing hell? You have persisted and insisted on visiting hell. I have personally led and showed you hell. From here on, I will take you more often. Throughout the world, it is a rare occasion to take a group to visit hell. We will now leave, so gather yourselves and follow me cautiously. Once Jesus finished speaking, the Pastor returned back to us in his normal body. We followed the Lord and began to leave hell. The Lord said, "If your mind wanders and you take your eyes off of Me, you will be in danger. Do not lose sight of Me! Gather yourselves and follow Me." We tensely walked in caution as we exited hell. We left hell.

April 17th, 2005 (Sunday Evening)

Sermon scripture: "For from within, out of the heart of men, proceed evil thoughts, adulteries, fornications, murders, Thefts, covetousness, wickedness, deceit, lasciviousness, an evil eye, blasphemy, pride, foolishness: All these evil things come from within, and defile the man." (Mark 7:21-23)

Pastor Kim, Yong-Doo: During these days, the Lord speaks to me frequently in dreams and through visions. "Pastor Kim, you are in lack of praying these days! You must pray a little more frequently and more fervently!" The Lord never allows us to be lack in praying. No matter what we are to do, we must always have prayer as our foundation — the Lord emphasized this to me. I was planning to finish my sermon a bit early today and go rest, but the Lord led me in a totally different direction.

Even though my physical body became unbearably tired, the Lord had come to us with a very special plan. We are always very grateful and thrilled when the Lord surprises us with presents. The Lord leads or brings circumstances that are unpredictable and He does continue to keep us in a state of astonishment. With the prayer and confession of the "Apostles Creed" at the beginning of service and through powerful worship, the Lord makes us into fireballs.

Worshipping in the fire brings indescribable joy and the Lord watches with more excitement. Jesus delightfully danced as we sang worship songs. He danced for about an hour. The Lord then said with a loud voice. "I will grant you special gifts. All of you come to the front and line up. Let us go to heaven as a group today!" Everyone shouted and cheered. "Yeah! Let us rejoice!"

* Visiting Heaven As A Group With the Lord

I asked the Lord: "Lord, I remember when you said you could only take one person to heave at a time." The Lord answered, "Yes I did. But you have made me very happy today. I want to take all of you to heaven as a group! Why are you complaining?" I replied, "No, not at all! I am not complaining! Rather, I thank you. However, there are some who have not had their spiritual eyes opened — how will they be able to see?" The Lord answered, "Do not worry about that because the saints with spiritual eyes can stand in line with the other saints who do not have their spiritual eyes opened. They are to stand in the order of every other non-spiritual opened eye saints. This way, the saints with spiritual eyes can explain about heaven." With that question, I continued to pry and ask many more questions, pointing out things that I was curious about. The Lord replied, "Pastor Kim, why are you being so religious? You have become so religious and now are used to it. Why don't you get out of that religious state and routine and give me true worship and service!" I was not able to say anything. I followed Him in silence.

The Lord requested, "I love the worship that your church gives me. I am very delighted, joyful, and astounded at your worship. Let us stop talking and follow me. Today, Pastor Kim will experience a special event. He will be preaching at the church in heaven. Preach with humor and bring the Father and I joy. Now, the heavenly spirits are very excited. They know a group of saints from the Lord's Church are coming to visit heaven. They are about to celebrate. They are clamoring to see you. They are preparing a great celebration! Pastor Kim will preach impressively. Until now, I was the only One who witnessed and visited you. Today, countless numbers of mighty angels and heavenly spirits will be listening to your sermon, in person. They will enjoy it. Pastor Kim, please preach as you preach on earth. Do not get nervous and freeze up, but freely, as you are. Make the Father, Holy Spirit, and I joyful!" I was reminded again. I asked Jesus, "Lord, I am not completely opened with my spiritual eyes. What kind of sermon do you want me to preach?" The Lord smiled and said that it will be all right.

Kim, Joseph: We continued to move forward toward heaven with Jesus at the lead. We passed the atmosphere and through space, and then came the galaxy. Joo-Eun shouted at the end of the line. "Wow! Pastor! We are at the galaxy!" This time Sister Baek, Bong-Nyu screamed, "It's the galaxy!" No matter how many times I may see it, the galaxy is always an amazing sight. It is magnificent and spectacular.

Jesus said, "All of you, hold your hands tightly! From here, we will be going into the dark tunnel." Whenever I pass through this dark tunnel, it feels so very cold and sobering. I also get goose bumps all over my body and I began to shake. I do not like this type of feeling at all. The Lord shouted, "My precious flock of sheep from the Lord's Church, you are truly pitiful and poor. Even in your difficult state, you are all devoted to prayer. Therefore, I will show you heaven and show you as much as you wish of heaven. We are almost there!" We arrived at heaven's gate. There was an unimaginable number of mighty angels and heavenly saints welcoming us. "Hallelujah! Wow! Welcome to heaven! It must have been a tiring trip coming all the way here to heaven. Oh, this saint is Freckles; I have been always hearing about you! Miss Mole! I see you again." Among the welcoming party, I could see some that I had already often met in heaven and some I had not seen before and was meeting for the first time. They welcomed and hugged us. They were busy greeting all of us.

First, we entered into the Father's throne and bowed down reverently. The Pastor said, "Father God, we who are full of sins are here. Please forgive our sins." Father said, "You must be tired from your trip. HaHaHa!" With His deep voice, He laughed in delight.

As soon as Father God and Jesus allowed us to converse with the heavenly saints, a multitude of saints converged on us to speak with us. In heaven, to delight God, four different special events had been planned. We were to lead the events. We seemed to have been very popular. But the Pastor seemed to be more the center of attraction out of our group.

There were many more heavenly saints gathered around the Pastor. They were eager to touch the Pastor's hand. On earth, many people chase movie stars and attempt to get their autographs. They become very excited and happy over an autograph. I felt we were in some type of similar situation. It was a situation recreated in heaven. I was very surprised. As I watched my Father speaking to Jesus, tears began to flow out.

"My beloved Jesus! On earth, I am a nobody. I am merely known only by a small church, as a Pastor. I am a Pastor who is not really leading a great ministry. I do not understand why the heavenly saints want to meet and clamor for us. I do not understand this moment," my earthly father stated. The Lord replied, "Angels have already recorded your services with a heavenly video recorder and being shown in heaven. Furthermore, your faces and all of your stories about you are written in the heavenly newspaper. I share the heavenly newspaper with all the heavenly saints. Therefore, you have all become popular."

As I witnessed the scene, I felt like I was in a dream rather than reality. The heavenly spirits told us that Jesus knows every single act and records them. He then explains to the heavenly spirits about us. There were multitudes of people of faith from the Bible who were preparing to meet us. We were also able to shake hands and hug one another of them.

I also met Pastor Kim, Young Gun who had come to our church the day before yesterday to preach at our church. He said, "Wow! Joseph, you have come here. Before I had come to heaven, I didn't know the Lord's Church was known greatly in heaven." We all laughed together and hugged each other. We were thrilled. I translated the conversation of Pastor Kim, Young Gun to my father. I checked to see how our other church members were doing. They were also busy conversing with countless numbers of heavenly saints.

I especially wanted to talk to Moses more than any other prophet or heavenly saint. I had previously made up my mind to meet him if I was ever to visit heaven. So I shouted, "Prophet Moses!" As soon as I shouted, Prophet Moses appeared and greeted me. "Welcome Saint Joseph! I do truly welcome you to heaven." Moses than gently nodded his head as a gesture of welcoming me. Moses continued and requested, "Please do not exalt me and do not call me Prophet Moses. Please call me Saint Moses."

Pastor and Moses greeted each other as well. Pastor said, "Moses, we have once met at God's sanctuary, correct?" Moses replied, "Ah ha! That is correct." Pastor stated, "We met in a secret room where the Ark of the Covenant is located. The Lord was there with us as well. I remember there were some other things in there, am I correct?" As soon as the Pastor spoke on that subject, Moses waved his hand in surprise and said. "Please, you must not talk about that place. That place is forbidden to speak about — God does not allow it! Please stop talking about it!" The pastor instantly stopped.

Pastor Kim, Yong-Doo: Through my son, Joseph, I was able to greet and speak with Pastor Kim, Young Gun who had already passed away many days ago. Pastor Kim, Young Gun entreated, "I over-exerted my physical body for the Lord. My wish for my life was to die on the altar during my sermon. I thought if my work was for the Lord, my over-exertion was a great act. However, I was wrong. When I turned 61, I passed away and arrived in heaven. I realized that my age was still good enough to continue working for the Lord. I managed my health irresponsibly and my life ended at 61. I realized it after I had come to heaven. Pastor Kim, Yong-Doo, do not abuse your health like I did. Take good care of your health. Continue the work I was ordained to do; save many souls and lead them to heaven. I beg you, do not be like me, please?" A countless number of heavenly saints touched my hands and body. Whenever they touched me, my body sensed their touch and my hands would move spontaneously.

We met countless numbers of people in heaven and conversed with them. We shook hands and we spent a long time greeting one another, just as we would on earth. The Lord, Himself, led us to different places in heaven to show us around. Only the people with opened spiritual eyes were able to witness what was happening. The other members were only able to partially feel the places with their body senses as we moved about. For instance, when the heavenly saints held our hands, tugged our clothes, or hugged us, we were able to clearly feel those senses.

* Conversations With Moses, Job, Samuel And Samson

Moses stayed at my side throughout the visit, which gave us a chance to discuss about many historical Biblical events. My son Joseph was the liaison between Moses and I. I asked, "Saint Moses, I have a quick temper and am easily angered. How did you manage to lead that many people to Canaan? When we look in Exodus 17:1-6, there was an incident in which you struck the rock and water flowed out. How did you feel about it?" Moses answered, "I had more problems than you pastors have now. I was also a quick tempered person. In fact, I do not want to discuss about anything that happened on earth with me."

Moses is truly a great saint. He is always humble, never exalting his good works. In fact, the other heavenly saints were also the same way. I attempted and continued to converse with Moses by asking him to explain some scriptures which I did not understand completely. I was wondering and expecting how he would answer my questions. However, every time I asked him a question, he would tell me that he did not desire to discuss about the things that had happened on earth.

After I had finished with Moses, I met Job. He is a man of faith. We had a good conversation. I said, "Saint Job! The words in Job, chapter 8 verse 7 are especially cherished by the saints on earth. Your beginnings will seem humble, so prosperous will your future be." The other church members and I use that verse regularly. Job responded, "Oh really?" I said, "How did you overcome so many trials and sufferings? You were great." He answered, "I did not do anything. Everything was accomplished through the grace of Father God."

I continued asking. "Saint Job, your life was so dramatic. You body was covered with worms and scabs (Job 7:5-6). You had painful sores from the bottom of your feet to the top of your head. You even took a piece of broken pottery and scrapped yourself with it (Job 2:7-8). I like to hear how you felt. I like to comfort the saints on earth who are suffering with trials with your words of encouragement." But Job persistently said that everything was done through the Lord's grace.

Once again, I asked Job about the event at the end of the chapter. "Your children all died by Satan's hand but you were blessed with more children. Were the next children from the wife that had cursed you or were they from another wife?" Job replied as if he were annoyed and asked why it was so important for me to ask such questions. I, therefore, ended my conversation with him with a last statement. "When He has tested me, I will come forth as gold." I explained to him that many ministers cherished that particular verse.

After Job, I conversed with Samuel. "Saint Samuel, I like the verse that states, 'As for me, far be it from me that I should sin against the Lord by failing to pray for you. And I will teach you the way that is good and right' (1 Samuel 1:13). I try to live up to that verse." Samuel replied with great joy. "Ah! Is that right? Thank you. Pray without ceasing. When you pray, an answer always comes."

I met and conversed with many souls from the Bible. Unfortunately, I could not feel the reality of heaven since I did not have my spiritual eyes opened and had to converse through Joseph. There was a big celebration in heaven since our church members were present. Jesus urged us. "Hurry, finish your conversations with the heavenly saints. Let us go and visit the different places in heaven. I have many places to show you." As a result, I was not able to ask about all the verses I had in mind. There were still verses I wanted to ask because I did not understand them. They were difficult verses and there were more than one interpretation to them on earth. I desired to obtain an explanation on the disagreements. I was only able to briefly shake the hands of the people of faith and had to say my farewells to them. As we said our farewells, we made a promise to each other to meet again.

During our farewells, I continued to ask questions to Paul, Enoch, Samuel, Moses, and Samson. With Samson, I pried with a question about his relationship with Delilah. I asked him how beautiful was Delilah that you had to reveal your secret. Samson stated that he did not wish to discuss this matter since it was very embarrassing. I had realized that I hit a sensitive issue and did not take his feelings into consideration. When I realized this, I had regretted my actions. Joseph said, "Pastor, please stop now! Samson is embarrassed and perplexed." I had finished the conversation with an awkward moment.

* The Entrance Door To The Fire

Jesus said, "Follow Me. Let us go to the entrance of the tunnel of fire. The tunnel is filled with Holy Blazing Fire." We followed the Lord as He commanded. I had previously asked a personal favor to the Lord for this trip to the tunnel. My request had now been granted. The Lord said, "Pastor Kim, since you are lacking prayer, you have to pray a little more in order to be led into the tunnel. Today, through your children and the church members who have their spiritual eyes opened, you will be able to ask questions about the Fire tunnel. We will only stand in front of the entrance of the tunnel and then return."

The Lord stood in the front of the entrance where the Holy Blazing Fire was filled. I stood behind the Lord. We all felt the blazing heat as it spewed out from the tunnel. The heat radiated onto our body in such force that we had to turn away from it. I asked the Lord, "Even if we just stand in front of the entrance, the heat is enormous. How will I be able to endure the heat? I do not see how I will be able to take it." The Lord replied, "Do not concern yourself with that. I will make it possible for you to endure the heat. In order for you to become a Fireball, you will have to enter into the Fire tunnel. Only then, will you be able to obtain a ministry of Fire. There are many areas filled with the Holy Blazing Fire. You will have to go through each stage one at a time. Therefore, be sure to prepare yourselves through much prayer. Keep yourselves in good physical health and strength. Do not forget my instructions."

* The Saints' Homes In Heaven Are Located In The Same Neighborhood

Kim, Joo-Eun: As Jesus showed our homes in heaven, He explained the details of each one. The Pastor's house was so tall that I was not able to see the top. Mrs. Kang, Hyun-Ja's home was slightly shorter than the Pastor's home. But her home was just as amazingly tall and wide.

I also saw the homes of Brother Haak-Sung; Sister Yoo-Kyung; Brother Joseph; Deaconess Shin; Jung Min; Mina; Saint Lee, Kyung-Eun and mine. Since Saint Lee, Kyung-Eun had just repented and come back to the Lord, her home had just been laid with the foundation which was made out of gold. It appeared that Jesus had made up His mind to show us many places in heaven. The Lord had moved the homes of the congregation of the Lord's church to one of the best areas in heaven. Now we would be able to live close together and be able to fellowship more often. It looked as though the homes got wider as they got built higher. The form reminded me of a flower called, "Morning Glory." However, some of the homes had different shapes as well.

The Lord gave us some free time to move about. Free time was also granted to the heavenly saints. I sat on the grass and rested. We then played and ran around as much as we wanted. We all began to scatter and visit the different places in heaven. The time on earth was pass midnight, but in heaven, it felt like time has stopped. There was no concept of time.

"But do not forget this one thing, dear friends: With the Lord, a day is like a thousand years, and a thousand years are like a day." (2 Peter 3:8)

* Preaching At The Church In Heaven

Sister Baek, Bong-Nyu: Jesus called and gathered all of us. He lined us up in one line and led us toward the church in heaven. After we had walked for some lengthy time, the Lord said, "All right, here is the church in heaven! The church is already filled with many souls. The mighty angels have come. Quickly, go in!" We quickly entered into the church.

Heaven's church was unimaginably big and magnificence. It was awesome and indescribable. Joseph and Joo-Eun were very impressed. They interjected as they looked in amazement at the size of the church. Pastor and his wife who did not have their spiritual eyes opened could not see what was going on. I asked the Lord, "Lord, if you completely open the spiritual eyes of the Pastor and his wife and give them an opportunity to preach, it would really be great. It was truly regrettable that they could not see."

The Lord said, "Pastor Kim and Mrs. Kang, Hyun-Ja will later have the deepest and greatest spiritual awakening. Although they are not able to currently see with their eyes, they will have to preach with enthusiasm and inspiration as usual."

It felt like the church of heaven is bigger than the whole earth. The church is not only filled with the heavenly saints but the angels are participating as well. With both parties, a great crowd is formed. Jesus went up to the altar where the Father's throne is located and He had all of us bow to the Father. We politely bowed and worshipped. We then bowed down to the ground.

As Jesus stood in front of the cross on the altar, He introduced each one of us to the heavenly saints. Jesus stood at the center of the altar. The first row, at the left, was taken by Moses. Angel Gabriel and Michael stood on each side, one to the left and right.

They had fixed their eyes on us. The Pastor went up to the altar and gave his salutation to the crowd. As songs continuously played, worship began. Just like our church, the people danced in the Holy Spirit and moved to the front. At the sound of worship, they danced. The songs that were sung were, "Receive Holy Spirit," "Up and Fight Against the Devil" and others. The songs continued which were about the Holy Spirit and then about the blood of Jesus.

It looked as though Mrs. Kang, Hyun-Ja's Holy Spirit dance had reached full maturity. She danced as water tranquilly flowed. She began to dance with power in which her motions transformed from tranquility to strength as the Holy Spirit poured Fire upon her. As she became heated by the Holy Fire, her face gradually turned red. The heavenly souls had fixed their eyes on Mrs. Kang, Hyun-Ja's Holy Spirit dance. As Jesus loudly laughed in delight, He was very satisfied. "Saint Kang, Hyun-Ja has completely fallen for Me." When we had service on earth, the Lord had brought the Prophet Elijah several times to our service. After our services, Elijah would approach Mrs. Kang, Hyun-Ja and state, "How are you able to so beautifully dance in the Holy Spirit? I love to see your hands." Elijah then touched her hands.

Mrs. Kang, Hyun-Ja danced in the Holy Spirit for a lengthy time. During the middle of her dance, the heavenly souls and angels enthusiastically shouted in cheers and all mingled together. They also danced and worshipped God together. The Pastor then came up to the altar and began preaching while Jesus watched on the side. When the Pastor preached, the heavenly souls laughed or listened seriously based on the Pastor's facial expression. He was preaching just as he preached on earth. He was humorous as usual. He even used his body gesture as he preached. Every time he gestured his body, there would be an explosive sound of laughter.

April 20th, 2005 (Wednesday)

Sermon scripture: "For the vision is yet for an appointed time, but at the end it shall speak, and not lie: though it tarry, wait for it; because it will surely come, it will not tarry. Behold, his soul which is lifted up is not upright in him: but the just shall live by his faith." (Habakkuk 2:3-4)

Pastor Kim, Yong-Doo: Our house has been sold from the auction. Since it has been sold, we have received dozens of phone calls on a daily basis. They wanted us out. They spoke to us in disrespect and threatened us with harsh language. We were leasing a home and had a deposit. Now, we were in danger of getting kicked out and losing our deposit. We had only one option left — we had to leave. It was just a matter of time. Today was the worst of worst days: we received our final notice by telephone. They had told us in one sentence, "Get out this week," and then they hung up. My heart was in agony and distress. I got dressed in my gym clothes and went out to the park for some fresh air. However, my heart was still heavily burdened.

* At the dinner table, we appealed to the Lord.

The Lord spoke through Joo-Eun. "Pastor Kim! In this situation, if your faith becomes weak, I will have to discipline you. The difficult trials you experience are nothing compared to the blessings you will receive in the future. Therefore, be patient and endure." After I had heard the words of the Lord, I was greatly strengthen and comforted. The Lord's word always gives me unspeakable joy, hope, and comfort.

"Now our Lord Jesus Christ himself, and God, even our Father, which hath loved us, and hath given us everlasting consolation and good hope through grace, Comfort your hearts, and stablish you in every good word and work." (2 Thessalonians 2:16-17)

* The Devil Devours And Chews A Person Whole

Kim, Joseph: Brother Haak-Sung and I held our hands together and followed Jesus to hell. Jesus said, "Joseph and Haak-Sung, you must tightly hold on to my hands! Today, I will show you the other place in hell." With Jesus in the center, we both held His hand on each side. As we walked the narrow path, we saw both sides of the narrow way. The maggots began to increase as high as mountains.

Even though, we held onto Jesus's hands, the maggots began to attack and stick on to us. Holding onto the Lord's hand tightly, we shouted, "Holy Fire" and then the maggots began to fall off. But when we did not hold on to the Lord's hands tightly, the maggots began to stick back onto us again. We passed that place and walked for some time when the Lord said, "Look in that direction!" When I turned my eyes to the direction where Jesus was pointing, I almost passed out from the sight.

There were a few demons who had enormous bodies. Their sizes appeared to be tens of thousands of times larger than humans. There were about five to six of them as they were very noisy from partying. The sounds of their voices reached us and could be clearly heard. My whole body was covered with goose bumps. There was also a black pot with people's blood. They had squeezed the blood from humans into the pot. The pot was filled with boiling blood. The color of the blood was dark red and was seething in heat.

There were countless number of people, all naked and bind. They were lined up next to the giants who were brutally torturing the people. As they waited for their turn, they screamed and shook in fear. The demons seized a few people with their enormous hands and then with their other hand, they would scratch the whole body to tear into the flesh. The blood drained better as the wounds were more severe. First, the blood was drained into the pot and then the demons would begin to eat the people, beginning with their head as they were still alive. The peoples" scream would soar into the skies of hell. "Ah! Help me! Please leave me alone! Devils. Demons. Ah!!" The devil was not interested in the peoples" screams or pleas. Every time the demons would eat the people alive, I could hear the sound which reminded me when we chew on chicken cartilage. "Wow! Delicious! I can't believe how delicious it is!" They were eating like ill-mannered creatures, making awful sounds as they ate the people alive.

Next, from the boiling pot, they poured the blood into the glass cups. They would toast one another and drink. "Hey! These are truly happy days. Let us drink as much as we want!" They were drunk by the blood of their victims. Toasting their cups, they laughed. For quite awhile, they enjoyed and laughed.

In fear, brother Haak-Sung and I told the Lord, "Jesus! These demons are so scary. We cannot bear the fear. We are no longer able to watch. What if they drag us as well?" The Lord comforted us. "It will be all right for I am with you." The demons would sometimes glance toward us as they chatted among with one another. Each time they looked at us, we became very nervous, but with the Lord next to us, we felt safe and were able to bear the frightening situation.

The demons appearance looked a lot like the ones that are easily found in illustrated storybooks. They had a horn on their head with one large eye in the center of their forehead. They looked like one-eyed goblin monsters. After they had eaten for awhile and had their fill, they appeared very satisfied and full. They held a club in their hand and laid on their backs to the floor. It didn't seem they would wake up in any short time. As brother Haak-Sung and I became very frightened, we did not know what to do. So in the midst of fear, we dug our faces into Jesus.

Within that moment, from the throne of Father God came a scroll. As soon as Jesus looked at it, He instantly took us to heaven.

Saint Lee, Kyung-Eun: I had not prayed in tongues for a long time. But now as I prayed in tongues, my tongue suddenly rolled backward and began to suffocate me. Then I was covered all over with a cold seat and soaked as if rained poured on me. I thought to myself, 'Ah! This is how people die from suffocation.' As I struggled and squirmed, I was able to barely breathe. I then began to repent. I did not know, but the pastor had already known I was having difficulty breathing. He came and laid his hands on me and prayed. As soon as the Pastor prayed, my tongue became normal and I had just avoided suffocation. Miss Kang, Hyun-Ja and Sister Baek, Bong-Nyu sat behind me and they were interceding on my behalf. I had not attended church for a long time. I had left the Lord for a long time and now I had returned. I once had received all kinds of Holy gifts in which I used to perform. Now, I return with all gifts terminated. For a long time, the loss of gifts had been the result of deception by the evil spirits. My will and thoughts were associated with the devils in so many areas and I was now confessing it. Today, I was determined to live my life in faith and before God. Therefore, the evil spirits were persistently clinging onto me with all their strength. But this incident made my faith more determined and stronger in willing to get ready to walk with God.

The events that are being revealed at the Lord's Church are difficult to find at other churches. These experiences shocked me. With the spiritual eyes of church members opened one by one, I could see that their focus was purely on the Lord. As I looked upon them, I was very embarrassed with my faith. I had thought my faith was strong and I was walking passionately. First thing for me was to restore my first love. So I repented in tears.

"I say unto you, that likewise joy shall be in heaven over one

sinner that repenteth, more than over ninety and nine just persons, which need no repentance."
(Luke 15:7)

WILL CONTINUE IN BOOK NUMBER FOUR...

Made in the
USA
Monee, IL